# Acknowledgments

Since first beginning research on First Lady history more than a dozen years ago, I have accumulated a long list of debts. Some of them were acknowledged in earlier publications, but one of them, to Susan Rabiner, who originally persuaded me to undertake the topic, deserves a repeat mention. She has remained a valued counselor, even when the study of presidents' wives took me in directions neither she nor I had anticipated. Betty Monkman, Associate Curator at the White House, read the entire manuscript and offered many helpful suggestions. Her mastery of White House history is a national treasure. Carl Sferrazza Anthony continues to share his encyclopedic knowledge of First Ladies; Judy Edelhoff directed me to huge files of photographs at the National Archives; Elise Kirk answered questions about music at the White House.

At the Smithsonian Institution, Polly Willman, Costume Conservator, opened her extensive slide collection, and shared her insights into what the clothes told about the woman. Edith Mayo and Kathryn Henderson offered suggestions culled from their years of experience with the First Ladies exhibit.

The various presidential libraries and sites are rich sources for documenting the history of chief executives' families—and the nation. Several archivists took time from busy schedules to meet with me: Philip Scott, at the Lyndon Baines Johnson Library; Steve Branch at the Ronald Reagan Library; Kevin Cartright at the Richard Nixon Library; Lou Knox at the Coolidge Room in the Forbes Library; Wallace Dailey, Curator of the Theodore Roosevelt Papers at Harvard's Houghton Library; Kelly Gagner at the Warren Harding House; Gil Gonzales, at the Rutherford Hayes home; Frank J. Aucella at the Woodrow Wilson House, and Ruth Corcoran, at the White House Historical Association.

The entire team at Doubleday Direct has been incredibly supportive. To Barbara Greenman goes credit for promoting the book at the beginning. Karen Murgolo, who had the difficult job of editing the entire project at a time of enormous technological change, performed with remarkable competence and uncommon grace. Eric Hafker cheerfully tracked down hundreds of photographs, even when the leads were slim. Dana Adkins, at Reader's Digest, offered many good suggestions.

Livio Caroli acted again as chauffeur, critic, and cheerleader—as he has for thirty years on four continents.

To all of them, I am grateful—far more than a brief mention here can show.

A small, prestigious sorority gathered in December, 1992 for the dedication of the Ronald Reagan Library. It was Pat Nixon's last public appearance. *(overleaf)*

Lady Bird Johnson     Nancy Reagan     Rosalynn Carter

Pat Nixon     Barbara Bush     Betty Ford

Adams 1797-1801 ⋆ Dolley Payne Todd Madison 1809-1817

hnson Adams 1825-1829 ⋆ Anna Symmes Harrison 1841 ⋆

Tyler 1844-1845 ⋆ Sarah Childress Polk 1845-1849

Fillmore 1850-1853 ⋆ Jane Means Appleton Pierce 1853-1857 ⋆

Johnson 1865-1869 ⋆ Julia Dent Grant 1869-1877

881 ⋆ Frances Folsom Cleveland 1886-1889 and 1893-1897 ⋆

Kinley 1897-1901 ⋆ Edith Carow Roosevelt 1901-1909

1913-1914 ⋆ Edith Bolling Galt Wilson 1915-1921 ⋆

Coolidge 1923-1929 ⋆ Lou Henry Hoover 1929-1933

uman 1945-1953 ⋆ Mamie Doud Eisenhower 1953-1961 ⋆

r Johnson 1963-1969 ⋆ Patricia Ryan Nixon 1969-1974

h Carter 1977-1981 ⋆ Nancy Davis Reagan 1981-1989 ⋆

Clinton 1993- ⋆ ⋆ ⋆ ⋆ ⋆ ⋆ ⋆ ⋆ ⋆

# AMERICA'S
## First Ladies

# AMERICA'S
## First Ladies

### BETTY BOYD CAROLI

DOUBLEDAY DIRECT, INC.
GARDEN CITY, NEW YORK

After leaving the White House, Eleanor
Roosevelt became known as "First Lady of
the World." *(above)* Lady Bird Johnson takes a
break from her official duties as First Lady to
wheel her grandson on the South Lawn of
the White House, August, 1967. *(page ii)*

Designed by Margaret Hinders

Art Direction by Nanna Tanier for Doubleday Direct, Inc.

Printed in the United States of America

Published by GuildAmerica Books®, an imprint and a registered trademark of

Doubleday Direct, Inc., Dept. GB, 401 Franklin Avenue,

Garden City, New York 11530

ISBN: 1-56865-168-6

# Contents

FOREWORD *ix*

CHAPTER ONE: *Family Woman* 1

CHAPTER TWO: *"Associate President"* 39

CHAPTER THREE: *Keeper of the White House* 83

CHAPTER FOUR: *Leader of Women* 129

CHAPTER FIVE: *After the White House* 175

APPENDIX 207

FURTHER READING 215

PHOTO CREDITS 215

INDEX 216

# $\mathcal{F}$oreword

Since that May day in 1789 when Martha Washington stepped off the presidential barge at the tip of Manhattan to join her husband, Americans have shown great interest in their presidents' wives. Martha quickly became the subject of letters to newspapers and discussions in the city's salons. Even the most inconsequential of her actions courted scrutiny. When the cream in her trifle dessert was judged a bit rancid, one critic suggested that she buy herself a cow. As for the title that she would be known by, consensus developed slowly. Some Americans favored "Lady," and others preferred "Marquise."

In the decades that followed, the nation's curiosity about leaders' spouses continued to grow. When the capital moved to the federal district on the Potomac, only the local population could observe a First Lady's every move. But Washington City housed representatives from the various states, as well as local folk, and they relayed their reactions to constituents at home. How a president's wife entertained and decorated the executive mansion, how she disciplined her children and cared for her parents, what she told the president and confided to her friends—all provided subject for observation and argument.

By the time the Civil War ended in 1865, presidents' wives had become national figures, partly because new magazines distributed across the land began to carry articles about the latest White House family. Their pets and eating habits, their in-laws and sleeping arrangements, were described (and sometimes pictured) in periodicals. Reports of Mary Lincoln's pregnancy (although false) and Julia Grant's difficulties with a precocious son (although mild) found their way into print. When Lucy Hayes traveled with Rutherford to the West in the summer of 1880, she became a national heroine, and it was during her tenure that the title, "first lady," found its way into print.

Martha Washington carefully set precedents that would last for two centuries. Her portrait—completed in the 1870s to accompany the famous portrait of George Washington—hangs in the East Room.

The title failed to gain a strong foothold until 1911 when a play, *First Lady,* became popular. The plot of Charles Nirdlinger's drama has little to do with the job of presidential spouse, although action centers around Dolley Payne Todd and the boarding house she ran in Philadelphia before she married James Madison. In the play, Dolley's good-hearted, natural style wins the approval of most Americans, but foreigners are not so kind: when word gets out that she has consented to marry James Madison, one British visitor snootily refers to her as "a former landlady." Perhaps that is the point of the play—that a woman of humble origins can serve successfully as the nation's "First Lady."

Not all who held the title liked it, and Jacqueline Kennedy forbade her staff to use it. She thought it sounded more like a "saddle horse" than consort to the president of the United States. "But finally, we just gave up," her social secretary, Letitia Baldrige, admitted. "Too many people had become accustomed to it."

By the 1980s, the title had taken firm root in the United States and spread to other nations. Italians absorbed it into their language without translation (to refer to the wife of their president), and Russians attached it to Raisa Gorbachev. From the Philippines to Haiti, newspaper headlines described their own "First Lady."

What initially drew Americans to their presidents' families has never been fully explained. Perhaps the loss of a queen after independence left a void; or perhaps democracies encourage access to their leaders' lives in a way that other forms of government do not permit. In the twentieth century, television nurtured the public's illusion of intimacy with occupants of the President's House, and by the 1960s, millions of Americans knew not only the names of Jacqueline Kennedy's two children, but also that of Caroline's pony, Macaroni.

By then it had become clear that a president's spouse held potentially powerful access. Unappointed and unelected, she benefited from a Constitution that allows a chief executive great freedom to choose

Caroline Kennedy's pony, Macaroni, became a national favorite. *(above)* On her trip through Europe in 1919, Edith Wilson (seated at left) was often compared to royalty. *(opposite)*

Frances Folsom, aged twenty-two, attracted enormous attention when she married forty-nine-year-old President Grover Cleveland in 1886. *(above)* Two decades after leaving the White House, Jacqueline Kennedy Onassis met First Lady Nancy Reagan. *(opposite)*

advisers, unlike the parliamentary system that ties a prime minister closely to a political party. Husbands who valued their wives' judgments have turned to them for counsel, and almost from the beginning of the Republic, America's First Ladies experimented with the limits of their "derived" power. When John and Abigail Adams showed how a strong marriage partnership could help shape a presidency, her critics dubbed her "Mrs. President."

The tradition that a chief executive kept his office at home also enhanced his wife's influence. She could hardly remain oblivious of political intrigue when so much of it played out under her nose. Official visitors from all over the world passed through the family's quarters. Entertaining, even on relatively private occasions, had its public, political side. A First Lady's preferences in fashion, food, art, and entertainment reflected on the entire nation, and she heard herself chastised for lapses and lauded for success.

Because of her conspicuous role, the First Lady became a model for other American women who have traditionally found their heroines closer to home, in the form of mothers, aunts, and schoolteachers. White House occupants watched as women across the continent copied their hairstyles and borrowed their names. For some presidential consorts, the attention was extremely embarrassing, especially when the stories were false. During Grover Cleveland's 1888 campaign for reelection, rumors circulated that he abused his young wife, and she received a letter asking if the charges were true. Frances Cleveland replied in a public letter that these were "wicked and heartless lies" and she could only hope for her countrywomen that "their homes and lives may be as happy and their husbands may be as kind, attentive, considerate, and affectionate as mine."

Frances Cleveland survived her White House tenure by fifty years, and she learned, as would her successors, that the First Lady continues to play a leadership role long after her husband's official term ends. Pat

Nixon left Washington in 1974, and after suffering a stroke two years later, she rarely made public appearances or gave interviews. Yet she continued to make *Good Housekeeping*'s list of "Most Admired Women in America," into the 1990s.

Even the most popular presidential spouses have their critics, and censure is particularly harsh for activist, strong First Ladies. Eleanor Roosevelt, who illustrated the enormous potential in the job, was ridiculed for her looks as well as her actions, and Hillary Rodham Clinton, whose husband billed her as his full partner, was held up to equal disparagement. One cartoonist suggested impeaching Lady Bird Johnson.

A fortunate by-product of all the attention focused on 1600 Pennsylvania Avenue is a huge cache of pictorial images. Except for the elusive Margaret Taylor, of whom no accurate picture survives, each president's spouse was painted or photographed, and many were caricatured and cartooned. This book is drawn from the myriad images available, and it attempts to show the enormous variety in America's First Ladies over more than two hundred years.

A popular First Lady for the 1950s, Mamie Eisenhower later admitted that she was not expected to do the public speaking that her successors took for granted.

# Family Woman

The most visible woman in America—the president's wife—cannot ignore her family without

paying a price. Husbands—even those at the top of the political ladder—may flaunt their relatives or

disregard them, but a First Lady has less choice. Whatever else she accomplishes, she will be scruti-

nized and judged for how she mothers her children,

cares for her parents, sustains her siblings, and supports

her spouse. Although an enormous legacy of activism

Hillary Rodham Clinton insisted that daughter Chelsea (at left) be kept out of the limelight. *(opposite)* Ellen Wilson (second from right) married two of her daughters out of the White House—Eleanor (far left) and Jessie (far right). *(above)*

*1*

Sarah Polk, who had no children, accompanied her husband to Washington for congressional sessions.

and accomplishment survived her, Eleanor Roosevelt is still remembered by many Americans as "a mess as a mother" (while few paid any attention to Franklin's record as a father).

More than one president's wife publicly acknowledged her family duties. Lady Bird Johnson spoke of making "a comfort area, an island of peace" so her husband could do his "best work." The highly professional and accomplished attorney Hillary Rodham Clinton introduced herself to a congressional committee as "a mother, wife, sister, a woman," and Jacqueline Kennedy, for all her emphasis on glamour and style, stressed her primary responsibility to her family. "If a woman fails at raising her children," she often said, "then nothing else much matters."

## Childless First Ladies

Being childless lessened family obligations—as Sarah Polk, wife of James K. Polk (1845–1849), demonstrated. During the years her husband served in Congress, she routinely left Tennessee at the beginning of each legislative session and accompanied him to Washington. He evidently liked having her with him because, when she suggested she stay home to look after the house, he chided her: "Why? If the house burns down, we can live without it." Educated at one of the best academies in the nation, Sarah had a fine mind, and after marrying James when she was twenty-one, she concentrated her energies on helping him. Not all his colleagues approved, and some of them muttered that she dominated him. Just as the Polks were preparing to move into the White House in 1845, Vice President-elect George Dallas wrote his wife a mixed endorsement of the new First Lady: "She is certainly mistress of herself and I suspect of somebody else also."

Sarah put little stock in building a reputation as excellent household manager. When one man volunteered that he was going to vote for James K. Polk's opponent Henry Clay because Mrs. Clay made better butter, Sarah retorted that her husband would win anyway, adding that when she got to the White House she did not expect to make butter at all, but live comfortably on the $25,000 salary the president then earned.

## Large Families in the White House

Large families could complicate First Ladyship, and some presidential families were enormous by twentieth-century standards. The most prolific chief executive, John Tyler, eventually fathered fifteen children (by two wives), eight of them born before he took the oath of office in 1841. By then only the four youngest, ranging in age from eleven to eighteen, required much parental attention, but the older ones stayed close at hand and, in the style of the time, resided in the executive mansion.

First Lady Letitia Tyler (1841–1842) had suffered a stroke two years before moving into the White House (where she died a year later), so her daughter-in-law, Priscilla Cooper Tyler, performed most of the hostess duties in her place. Daughter of a popular Shakespearean actor, Priscilla had appeared on stage before her marriage to the Tylers' son and received excellent reviews. Accustomed to the limelight, she found the executive mansion a fitting stage for performances of a different kind. "Here I am actually living in and, what is more, presiding at the White House," Priscilla wrote her sister in 1841, "and I look at myself . . . and exclaim 'Can this be I?'"

Almost half a century later, Caroline Harrison (1889–1892) repeated much of Letitia Tyler's experience: she brought a large extended family to live at the White House, and she died there shortly before her husband's term ended. Her two children were both grown and married with children of their own before Benjamin became president in 1889, and Caroline invited them and their families, as well as her aged father and a widowed niece, to live in the eight rooms then set aside for the chief executive's family on the second floor.

Not surprisingly, Caroline Harrison decided she needed more space,

**Actress Priscilla Cooper Tyler often substituted for her ailing mother-in-law as White House hostess.**

The grandchildren of Caroline and Benjamin Harrison became favorite subjects for photographers, both amateur and professional, in the 1890s.

and she worked with a family friend, the engineer Frederick Owen, to develop plans to enlarge the White House. Drawings for the proposed changes show additions on both sides of the mansion that would have made it a huge quadrangle, with one wing serving as a museum. Unfortunately for Caroline, a balky Congress refused to appropriate the funds, and she had to make do with the same 165-by-85-foot structure that had served presidential families since 1800.

The Harrisons thrived on public attention, at least in the beginning of the administration. Caroline Harrison shopped in Washington stores and encouraged other members of the family to mingle with the public as much as possible. The president's young grandson, Benjamin McKee, outdid all the adults in gaining press coverage. Dubbed the most photographed child in America, he was singled out by a staff member as "one of the principal personages of the White House" although he was only two years old.

## Mothers of Young Children

Only a handful of First Ladies took their own young children to live in the White House, but those who did delighted the nation. In any contest for the most popular young family, contenders would certainly include Julia Grant's lively brood of four, Frances Cleveland's bewildered toddlers, Edith Roosevelt's rambunctious gang of six, and Jacqueline Kennedy's photogenic duo. Each family had its turn in the national spotlight, and none of them—child or mother—was ever quite the same again. Millions of Americans came to look on these youngsters as national mascots—and insisted on helping to raise them—chuckling at their antics and clucking in disapproval when they misbehaved.

By the 1960s, ubiquitous cameras and reporters made a protective mother's job more difficult. Jacqueline Kennedy (1961–1963) tried to ration the photographic opportunities for daughter Caroline, three years old when they moved into the White House, and son John, born just two months before. She refused to reveal the name of the diaper supplier or the location of the baby's nursery, and when reporters got too close, infringing on the privacy she thought necessary for raising healthy children, she appealed to her husband's press secretary, Pierre Salinger, for help. "If you are firm and will take the time, you can stop it," she wrote him on one of her long yellow memo sheets. "So please do . . . protect us." Caroline picked up her mother's attitude and at age five was known to walk past reporters, muttering, "No photographers!"

Rather than send her young daughter out to nursery school, Jacqueline Kennedy established a classroom on the top floor of the executive mansion and invited several of Caroline's young friends to join her there. By the fall of 1963, the children were doing first-grade work, and when the president was assassinated in November, one of the First Lady's considerations was how to finish the school year. Her successor, Lady Bird Johnson, insisted that the classes continue until the previously scheduled Christmas break; so for a month after the Johnsons had moved

Her son, John, ignored most of Jacqueline Kennedy's fashion statements—but not her pearls. *(above)* Rosalynn Carter's daughter, Amy, was only nine when Jimmy became president. *(below)*

On a summer trip to Italy in 1962, Jacqueline Kennedy and daughter Caroline (on her lap) were warmly welcomed. *(above)* Back in the White House, Caroline celebrated a birthday. *(opposite)*

into the residence, young Caroline and her friends trooped up to the school room daily to continue their routine.

School was not yet a consideration for son John (known to the nation by his baby name "John-John"). He was only three when his father died. Indeed, his third birthday fell on November 25, the day his father was buried, and the grieving First Lady had to fit in that family milestone around meetings with world leaders who had come for the state funeral and preparations to move out of the White House. The birthday party was not held until December 6, but, as any mother knows, a child's birthday cannot go unmarked, no matter how huge the personal tragedy or the political crisis that coincides with it.

As First Lady, Jacqueline Kennedy tried to make her children's lives as much as possible like those of their less famous friends. Caroline rode her pony, Macaroni, on the White House lawn and competed in a pony rally in nearby Virginia. But hers was hardly an ordinary childhood. She punctuated the most solemn occasions—giving the president a kiss during one of his speeches and interrupting a twenty-one-gun salute for an important international visitor by shouting out with her friends. Much as the outburst amused reporters, the children were hustled out of sight.

Summers away from the capital gave the Kennedys little relief from publicity. When Jacqueline took Caroline with her to Ravello, Italy, in August 1962, she hoped for a relaxed private holiday with her sister, Lee Radziwill. But photographers followed her every outing to water ski or yacht or swim. Like others who had preceded her to the White House with young children, the First Lady pursued a balancing act—how to mother her children in the way she wished without offending a curious public.

By the 1960s, television tended to encourage popular fascination with presidential families, but First Ladies had complained much earlier of the difficulties of trying to raise young children in full view of millions. Frances Cleveland (1886–1889; 1893–1897), who married Grover

Frances Cleveland, the only president's wife to give birth in the White House, is shown with daughters, Ruth (at left) and baby Esther.

in the middle of his first term and then had to move out of the White House when he lost the election of 1888, returned in 1893, after he had won a second term, with their eighteen-month-old daughter, Ruth, in tow. Six months later Frances gave birth to a second daughter, Esther, the first child of a president to be born in the White House. Before Grover finished his second term, the Clevelands had a third daughter, Marion.

Three little girls running or being pushed in their prams around the lawn at 1600 Pennsylvania Avenue proved enticing subjects for amateur photographers. By the 1890s, many Americans owned inexpensive Kodak cameras, and when they toured Washington, they wanted to take home a souvenir snapshot from the President's House. Some tourists insisted on getting even closer: one day, as baby Ruth was being taken for a walk by her nurse, Frances Cleveland was appalled and frightened to see a total stranger lift the child out of her carriage.

The man was harmless, but Frances and the president decided to make other living arrangements. They rented a house called "Red Top" a few miles away, where the family had a magnificent view of the Potomac and Grover could escape what he called the "cursed, constant grind." Although the Clevelands returned to the White House for official entertaining, they were ridiculed for isolating their youngsters, and stories persisted that the girls were deformed or ill.

When Theodore Roosevelt suddenly became president after the assassination of William McKinley in 1901, the usually unflappable Edith Roosevelt appeared to have her hands full. In addition to her irrepressible seventeen-year-old stepdaughter, Alice, Edith had five children of her own, ranging in age from fourteen-year-old Theodore Jr. down to four-year-old Quentin. But for two miscarriages—each of them duly noted in newspaper gossip columns when she had to withdraw abruptly from social engagements—she would have given birth to two more in the White House.

During Theodore's two terms, his family underwent many changes, as the older boys went off to boarding school and Alice married a prominent congressman. When young Theodore, at school in Groton, Connecticut, came down with pneumonia, Edith dropped everything to go nurse him. For thirty-six tense hours he lay close to death, but he pulled through and recovered sufficiently to return with her to Washington to convalesce.

The health of the president's children was national news, and Edith's mothering was complicated by a desire to exclude the press from what she considered private family matters. She had already developed some skill in coping with reporters' intrusions. When the family dog, Jack, died, she wired the boys so they would hear the sad news from her rather than read about it, with the rest of the nation, in the newspapers.

With more success than Caroline Harrison had enjoyed, Edith Roosevelt took up the cause of enlarging the living quarters for the president's family. Theodore's talk of the presidency providing a "bully pulpit" helped focus attention on the chief executive, and Congress was finally persuaded that TR could hardly be expected to house his family on one side of the second floor and operate out of cramped offices down the hall. Within a year of moving in, the Roosevelts had permission to call in the distinguished architectural firm of McKim, Mead, & White to renovate the residence and construct an attached but separate office building (later called the West Wing), thus freeing up the entire second floor for the presidential family.

Even when the enlarged quarters were complete, the energetic Roosevelt children still romped through the whole house. Teenaged Alice, who delighted in shocking staid Washington society, went up to the roof to smoke cigarettes. Her siblings took advantage of the high-ceilinged public rooms on the first floor to try their skills on stilts. Edith's youngest, Quentin, won most attention when he took a pony up to the second floor on the elevator. His brother Archie had been sick, and Quentin decided a visit from his pony would cheer him up. Their antics

Edith Roosevelt (seated beside her husband, Theodore) hoped formal portraits would appease public curiosity about her children. Left to right: Theodore, Jr., Archie, Ethel, Quentin, and Kermit.

Lynda Bird Johnson (at left) graduated from her mother's alma mater, the University of Texas. *(above)* Betty Ford, seated between her son and daughter, learned that teenagers have their own problems with White House living. *(opposite)*

endeared the young Roosevelts to Americans, and Edith met numerous demands for photographs by distributing formal posed pictures of herself and the children. She hoped her strategy would satisfy reporters and decrease the chances they would camp out on the steps or follow the youngsters to school in anticipation of getting a candid shot. In any case, she avoided the kinds of rumors that Frances Cleveland faced about her children.

## Teenagers in the White House

By the time she left Washington in 1909, Edith's children, except for Quentin, were all in their teens, but she had learned, like other First Ladies before and since, that teenagers have their own particular struggles living in the White House. The chance to meet world leaders and other celebrities cannot always compensate for the disadvantages of residing in what some have called the "glass square." Grace Coolidge (1923–1929) heard her teenaged son explain to his father that he would be late for dinner and would not have time to dress. Calvin Coolidge paused and then informed him: "You will remember that you are dining at the table of the president of the United States, and you will present yourself promptly in proper attire."

Lady Bird Johnson (1963–1969) had two daughters already familiar with public life when Lyndon became president—he had served many years as Senate leader and vice president—and older daughter Lynda had already judged Washington to be a place that was "great for congressmen and their wives but terrible for the children." She found difficulties in the White House, perhaps because her mother frequently reminded her that many people were watching. Standard instructions for preparing for a state dinner included advice to read up on the country of the honored guest and "not touch the wine."

Much as she wanted both girls to have the rare opportunities of life at 1600 Pennsylvania Avenue, Lady Bird understood that her daughters,

like most teenagers, insisted on deciding important things for themselves, no matter where their father worked. Luci continued to go to the National Cathedral School, but Lynda had already enrolled at her mother's alma mater, the University of Texas—too far away to spend much time at the White House. Lady Bird could only wait, and it came as "a delight" and "the surprise of the evening," she wrote in her diary, when Lynda stood up at a small dinner party and announced that she wanted to transfer to George Washington University. She had decided to leave the school with the "number one football team in the nation" to live in the house where she "could listen to the number one people."

Although Lynda later transferred back and graduated from Texas in 1966, she and her sister continued to get a lot of the nation's attention. Not all of it was welcomed. Luci Johnson later described how she felt: "Slam bam and that was it, we were in the White House. I had just gotten my driver's license and my first car and all of a sudden I had a twenty-four-hour chaperone." Both girls dated (sometimes disguised in wigs and dark glasses), married, and gave birth to their first child while their mother presided over the White House.

Although extremely busy with her own projects and the job of overseeing the White House, Lady Bird worked to keep open communication channels with her daughters. Except for the times when she hung a tiny pillow on her doorknob, saying "I want to be alone," they were always welcome. Lynda later wrote for *McCall's* magazine how she had gone into her mother's bedroom in the "very early hours" to share the news that she had just agreed to marry White House social aide Captain Charles Robb.

For the Johnsons, as for most presidential families, the White House was the culmination of a long career that took the politician away from his family for much of the year, leaving his wife in charge at home. First Ladies are usually seasoned at single parenting. During Gerald Ford's long career in the House of Representatives, where he had to campaign every two years, Betty Ford, who had four children within seven years, learned to deal with many minor crises on her own. She later joked that she had driven to the local emergency room so often that the car could make the trip on its own. Privately, she may have resented such heavy responsibility; she once said that if her children were asked which parent had influenced them most, they should certainly point to her because "their father was always away."

Perhaps because her husband got to be president without running in a national campaign, Betty Ford tended to be more candid than most First Ladies in discussing her teenagers with reporters. She explained her bluntness by saying she thought people were tired of cover-ups after the Watergate revelations, but whatever the reason, she gained a reputation for saying just what she thought without calculating the political fallout. On national television, she speculated that her sons had experimented with marijuana, and she volunteered that she might have tried it herself if it had been popular when she was young.

A comment about her eighteen-year-old daughter, Susan, brought even more attention. When Betty was asked on *60 Minutes* what she would do if she learned that Susan was having an affair, Betty replied that she would not be surprised and then went on to suggest that premarital relations with the right partner might lower the divorce rate.

Reaction to the frank First Lady varied. Americans who watched her on television generally approved, but those who saw her quoted in the next morning's newspapers responded more negatively. The president joked that he had originally calculated she had cost him ten million votes but had doubled the damage after reading printed accounts. A year later, however, polls showed Betty Ford's popularity stood higher than ever. She had successfully bridged the gap between the honesty that she valued and an old expectation, held by many Americans, that presidential families will pretend to be perfect. Her candor won her many admirers.

Lady Bird Johnson (at left) arranged White House wedding receptions for both her daughters. Here she is shown with older daughter, Lynda.

## White House Weddings

Susan Ford was still single when her parents moved out of the White House in 1977, but the two previous administrations had seen a spate of weddings—though not all the brides wanted a White House ceremony. Julie Nixon actually pushed the date up to December 1968 so that it would come before her father's inauguration, and Luci Johnson opted for a church wedding (with a reception at the executive mansion). But the older daughters in both families, Lynda Johnson and Tricia Nixon, were married in the White House, the first such weddings in more than half a century.

Both Lady Bird Johnson and Pat Nixon learned, as several of their predecessors could have told them, that White House weddings are more than family affairs. The entire nation begs to be included, and political concerns cannot be ignored. Tours of the executive mansion continue up to the last possible moment—this is, after all, public housing—and people's names appear on the guest list although neither bride nor groom has ever met them.

In 1820, when the United States had few firm rules for presidents' families, Elizabeth Monroe (1817–1825) struggled to develop some guidelines for marrying a daughter out of the White House. Her seventeen-year-old, Maria, had set her nuptials for March, when the capital's social season had not quite ended. As soon as word got out, dozens of diplomats and legislators residing in Washington made no secret of their desire to be invited. Both Maria and her mother wanted a small gathering of family and closest friends, but they had no precedent to cite. This was the first time a president's daughter had been married in the White House.

Anticipation in Washington grew so great that Elizabeth Monroe dispatched Secretary of State John Quincy Adams to set people straight. The First Lady would keep the guest list short, Adams explained, and invite those whom the family wanted, without regard for political impli-

Julia Grant's only daughter, Nellie, thirteen years old when the family moved into the White House, was married there five years later. *(above)* Nearly a century later, Pat Nixon (at left) danced with her new son-in-law, Edward Cox, after daughter Tricia (shown dancing with her father) was married in a Rose Garden ceremony. *(opposite)*

**Rosalynn and Jimmy Carter entertained grandchildren, James, Jason, and Sarah, in the Cross Hall at the White House.**

cations. But Elizabeth paid a price. Washingtonians boycotted her other parties and wrote her off as snobbish and aristocratic, which would have been a decided disadvantage if her husband had wanted to run for another term (which James Monroe did not).

Later presidential families who married daughters out of the White House had to set their own limits and struggle with the public's desire to know every detail. Julia Grant (1869–1877) barred reporters when her eighteen-year-old daughter, Nellie, married in 1874, but the newlyweds were hounded all the way to New York City, where they boarded a ship for their European honeymoon. In 1906, Edith Roosevelt had to use three separate entrances to accommodate the one thousand guests invited to her stepdaughter Alice's wedding to Representative Nicholas Longworth. Ellen Axson Wilson (1913–1914) kept her daughters' weddings small, giving her own precarious health as the reason, but reporters resorted to trickery to find out the destination of the wedding trips.

The length of the guest list presented a minor problem for Pat Nixon when she began planning for Tricia's wedding in June 1971, but she had other difficulties. Tricia decided on a Rose Garden ceremony. This was the first time that idyllic spot had ever been the setting for such an event, and by the time it was over, Pat Nixon probably understood why. Rain fell intermittently throughout the day, holding off only long enough in the late afternoon for the vows to be exchanged. Then everybody moved—with relief—into the East Room for the party.

## Grandchildren

Although the Nixons had no grandchildren before leaving Washington, other presidential couples have had to fit in backup parenting with all their other responsibilities when their adult children died or turned to them for help. This was the case for the very first woman on the job, Martha Washington, who, like Jane Pierce and Ida Saxton McKinley, had lost all her children by the time her husband took office as president.

Although she did not care to be called Grandmother, Mamie Eisenhower (at left) happily posed with her four grandchildren.

In Martha's case, only one of the four born of her first marriage to Daniel Parke Custis ever reached adulthood, and she and George had none. Her first two died young, and daughter Patty, never well, suffered epileptic seizures from the age of twelve and was dead at seventeen. Martha pinned all her hopes on her surviving son, John, which may partly explain why he turned out to be a bit lazy. John Custis married in 1774 when the independence movement was reaching a peak, but he never fought with the revolutionary forces commanded by his popular stepfather, General George Washington. In 1781, he contracted "camp fever" and died, leaving a wife and four children.

The youngest two, Nelly and a boy named for the commander in chief, were taken into the Washington household and raised by Martha, who lavished attention on them. While looking after her First Lady duties in Philadelphia, she made all the arrangements so that teenage

Nelly Custis would look the "best possible" at a ball she planned to attend at Mt. Vernon. Martha put together a package of feathers, tassels, and other finery, then worried whether or not it would make the five-day journey in time.

More than a century later, another First Lady—Lou Hoover (1929–1933)—found herself temporarily substituting as parent to her grandchildren. After her elder son, Herbert Jr., then in his mid-twenties, was diagnosed with tuberculosis in the fall of 1930, he rented a house in Asheville, North Carolina, for rest and recuperation. His wife went to stay with him but thought it prudent to leave their three children, ranging in age from six months to four years, with their grandmother in Washington. Until the following spring, the children did not see their father, although they spoke with him on the telephone, and Americans got used to reading articles like "Baby Joan 'Rules' the White House." When the First Lady accompanied granddaughter Peggy and her friends to a Washington zoo, the excursion made the front page of major newspapers.

Scholarly Lou Hoover—never a favorite with employees, who found her demanding and severe—brightened considerably around her grandchildren. In December, she planned a Christmas party for two hundred youngsters and, with the Great Depression deepening, encouraged guests to bring gifts for children whose parents had lost their jobs. Four decorated pine trees, the Marine Band, and a "Mrs. Santa Claus" that looked a lot like Lou Hoover turned the party into a huge success, and one employee judged it the most fun of any he had ever witnessed at the White House.

## Adult Children's Careers

Because First Ladies typically start on the job when they are at least fifty years of age (only fifteen have been younger), their children have already set out to make their own careers. Their mothers must confront the

dilemma: how to encourage their grown children to make their own way without too much concern for the magnifying lens the nation focuses on them because of their father's job, and at the same time how to encourage them not to do anything that would create problems for the president.

What might amount to a minor episode in the life of any other young person becomes national news if it involves a member of the First Family. Young people can hardly expect to be judged by the usual stan-

Before he ran for national office, Franklin Roosevelt (seated back row left) posed with his rather glum family, including his mother (center) and wife, Eleanor (back row right), who had recently learned of his extra-marital relationship with Lucy Mercer.

dards if their father occupies the presidency—a lesson that dancer Ronald Reagan Jr. and banker Neil Bush learned, as did several of Eleanor Roosevelt's children and aspiring singers Margaret Wilson and Margaret Truman.

This particular complaint of First Ladies—that their children are judged by a more rigorous standard than others are—goes back to Abigail Adams (1797–1801), who wrung her hands in dismay as she read reports about her eldest, John Quincy. According to opposition newspapers, young Adams took advantage of his relationship to the president and got a job beyond his capabilities, but as Abigail protested, the accounts both exaggerated his salary and demeaned his assignment. The papers even got his age wrong, making him out to be far younger than he actually was. Abigail wrote to her sister that she had expected to be "vilified and abused" herself, but she regretted that her children suffered, too.

When their offspring's marriages fractured or failed, presidential wives found themselves called on to explain. Most wisely refused to comment. Republican Barbara Bush made no statement when her only daughter, Dorothy, divorced her husband, moved to the capital, took a job, and eventually married a man rumored to be a Democrat—hardly a scandal, but a spicy tidbit for the press. When reporters went digging for news about the wedding, which took place at the presidential retreat at Camp David, they met firm resistance from the First Lady's press secretary, who had been instructed, "No press about the wedding—not one word."

When Eleanor Roosevelt's only daughter, Anna, left her first husband and was seen in the company of journalist John Boettiger, whom she later married in 1935, it was Eleanor who faced reporters' questions. That was only the beginning. While she was First Lady, Eleanor's five children obtained a total of four divorces: one each for Anna and James and two for Elliott; after she left the White House, they added nine more.

But Eleanor, whose own marriage had its difficulties, refused to condemn her offspring for changing partners. "She thought they were seeking happiness," her niece explained, "and she could not deny them that." Newswomen who covered the First Lady's weekly press conferences reported that Eleanor never appeared ruffled or uncomfortable except when asked an unfriendly question about one of her children. Then her voice would take on an edge.

## Death of Children

Having her offspring criticized and ridiculed, or watching their marriages flounder, pales in comparison with a First Lady's grief when she loses a child in the White House. Of the five presidential wives who mourned a son, each had a slightly different story and bore her enormous sorrow in a different way. At least two risked turning their grief against themselves as well as their husbands.

Abigail Adams had barely moved into the unfinished President's House when word reached her that her middle son, Charles, had died in New York at the age of thirty. She was hardly surprised. Three weeks earlier, when she had stopped to visit him on her way south from Massachusetts to Washington, she had found him an alcoholic wreck, bloated and deranged, and she realized she would never again see him alive. Even so, when word of his death came, she was overwhelmed by a mixture of grief and relief, and she wrote her sister, "Weep with me over the grave of a poor unhappy child who cannot now add another pang to those which have pierced my heart for several years."

Jane Pierce (1853–1857) vies for title to the saddest life of all presidents' wives. Although she had given birth to three sons, all had died by the time Franklin Pierce was inaugurated, and in her irrational grief, Jane tied the boys' deaths to Franklin's success. Her firstborn succumbed soon after birth, not an unusual occurrence in a time when one child in five died before the age of one. Her second son died at age four. Jane put all

Jane Pierce was grief-stricken when son Bennie (at left) was killed in a railroad accident.

Mary Lincoln had already lost two sons (including Willie, shown in portrait) when this picture was made. Tad (at right) died a few years later.

her hope in her last born—Benjamin, who was a healthy ten years old when his father was nominated for the presidency. Even her return to the Washington she hated would be brightened by Bennie's presence.

Jane Pierce had never masked her dislike for living in the capital. She blamed the constant partying for tempting her husband to drink more than he should, and during most of the time Franklin served in Congress, she remained with relatives in Massachusetts, trying different cures for various maladies and general depression. But she understood that Franklin's elevation to the White House would require her presence, and she dreaded the thought. When informed he had been nominated by the Democrats, she fainted, and throughout the campaign she prayed for defeat.

When Franklin's election was announced in November 1852, Jane tried to make the best of it. Her own family encouraged her. They had not approved when she married Franklin, thinking their own social position considerably superior to his; but now they reconsidered. The presidency had its own perquisites, even for Jane's staid New England family, and they urged her to try harder: she should not become "a source of sorrow and anxiety" when her husband needed "strength and consolation."

All Jane's resolve fell away when she saw her beloved Bennie die—a horrible death. The family was traveling in Massachusetts when their train derailed; Bennie was decapitated in front of her eyes. Consumed with grief, Jane refused to attend her husband's inauguration two months later, and she kept a darkened President's House when she finally moved in. Critics eventually lost their patience and muttered about the gloomy atmosphere around the chief executive.

If Jane Pierce was chastised for grieving too much and too long, Mary Todd Lincoln (1861–1865) received the opposite reproach. She had already lost one child before becoming First Lady. In 1850 four-year-old Edward had died of diphtheria, a disease that was particularly lethal for young children in a time when no cure for it existed. Mary doted on her three remaining sons, especially Willie, and tried to make their time in the White House as pleasant as possible. Even with a war ripping the nation apart, she admonished her staff to "let the boys have fun."

In addition to mothering, Mary Lincoln had social obligations, made more difficult by the war. Parties, planned to boost morale, could turn into ghostly spectacles if casualties suddenly mounted. The First Lady understood the risk she faced if she appeared oblivious of people's suffering. At the same time, she thrived on the attention reserved for the White House hostess, and she plotted carefully to make her receptions elegant and memorable.

Plans for a large party on February 5, 1862, went forward in spite of Mary's concerns for her twelve-year-old middle son. Willie had fallen ill, probably with typhoid, although that had not been diagnosed. (At the time, typhoid claimed third place among the "killer" diseases, resulting in fewer fatalities than tuberculosis but more than diphtheria.) Washington was practically an incubator for the deadly *Salmonella typhosa* during the Civil War, when people flocked into the city. Wounded Union soldiers came for treatment, and families arrived searching for news of men missing in battle. The District of Columbia's few sewage lines, overworked by the influx of people, ruptured and spilled into the Potomac, the source of the water supply for the White House and much of Washington.

Two weeks after the party, Willie died. Both his parents were overwhelmed with grief, and Mary Lincoln became so distraught, she could not even attend the funeral services. In fact, she vowed never again to set foot in either the upstairs bedroom where Willie had died or the Green Room, where he had been laid out. When she donned the black mourning jewelry and clothing then requisite for close relatives, some of her critics charged that she had spent too much, thus putting in doubt how

deep her grief really went. Other mothers, whose sons had died in battle, questioned whether she suffered as much as they. Six months later, when she switched to the "half mourning" colors of lavender and gray, criticism increased.

Unlike Mary Lincoln, considered among the most unstable and unpopular of all First Ladies, Grace Coolidge had few detractors. Known as a witty, ebullient partner for the laconic "Silent Cal," she joked with reporters and looked as though she were having fun most of the time. An accomplished mimic and a known animal lover, she made a remarkable wife for one of the least personable presidents in history.

But some of that gay spirit was lost forever in the summer of 1924. The Coolidges' younger son, healthy, exuberant, sixteen-year-old Calvin Jr., blistered his foot while playing tennis on the White House court in early July. He ignored this seemingly minor problem, developed blood poisoning, and within days, died. The entire Coolidge family went into mournful shock. Their surviving son canceled his plans for camp and stayed close to his parents that summer, as though their unity could ward off further harm.

Within weeks, Grace Coolidge stoically resumed her duties as First Lady, but friends reported a subtle change. She began writing poetry, some of which she later published in national magazines, and became more introspective and serious. When an artist painted her portrait, he captured a sadness in her that not everyone had seen, and when questioned, he explained: "I saw a look of quiet resignation."

The boy's death left a large mark on the nation's consciousness. For years, mothers would exhort their youngsters to wear socks with their shoes so as not to get a blister, lest they die "the way the Coolidges' son died." Grace dealt privately with the same questions that trouble any mother who loses a child—how could she have prevented the death, and why did it happen? Five years after young Calvin's death, she composed a memorial poem that was read at her own funeral nearly forty years

An unusually somber Grace Coolidge resumed her First Lady duties after her son's death in 1924.

later. It began: "You my son / Have shown me God./ Your kiss upon my cheek / Has made me feel the gentle touch / Of Him who leads us on. . . ."

Not until nearly four decades later would another First Lady lose a child. On August 7, 1963, Jacqueline Kennedy gave birth prematurely to a four-pound-ten-ounce baby boy whom she and the president named Patrick Bouvier. It was the first baby born to a chief executive in sixty-eight years, and the nation showed enormous interest. But his immature lungs weakened the infant, and two days later he died. Although she grieved for her baby, the First Lady struggled to resume a full schedule as soon as possible, and by November, she agreed to accompany the president on his fateful trip to Dallas.

## Looking after Parents

More often than children, it is parents whom First Ladies lose while in the White House. If only a handful of presidents' wives were less than forty years old, only another handful—Anna Harrison, Margaret Taylor, Florence Harding, and Barbara Bush—were over sixty. Thus, most were in those middle years when there is a greater chance of losing one's parents. Indeed, it is the rare administration that does not witness the death of a parent of either the chief executive or his wife. Americans can supply their own list in recent memory: Bess Truman, Mamie Eisenhower, and Nancy Reagan mourned their mothers, Hillary Rodham Clinton her father, and both Hillary and Barbara Bush had to help their husbands through the loss of a mother.

If the First Lady is an only daughter, she may feel particularly responsible for a parent's care in the final years, and even a daughter-in-law experiences special obligations. Abigail Adams missed her husband's inauguration in 1797 because she was tending his sick mother in Massachusetts. Hillary Rodham Clinton left important meetings on health care reform to sit at her father's hospital bed in Little Rock.

Hugh and Dorothy Rodham (shown with daughter Hillary) attended the 1992 Democratic convention, but within a year the First Lady's father died. *(above)* Soon after this picture was taken, Jacqueline Kennedy gave birth prematurely to a son, Patrick Bouvier, who survived less than two days. *(opposite)*

Nancy Reagan's mother, Edith Davis, lived her last years in Arizona.

Nancy Reagan's mother, once a saucy showgirl who had married a Chicago surgeon, was able to attend the inaugural lunch in 1981 and swap stories with House Speaker "Tip" O'Neill. But her condition quickly deteriorated, and Nancy explained, "There was no longer any communication, but at least I could touch her and kiss her." In fall of 1987, the First Lady delayed a scheduled visit to her mother in Phoenix when she discovered she would have to undergo surgery. Before she had fully recovered from the mastectomy, Nancy learned that her mother had died of a stroke. The resolve that had helped her through the operation now deserted her, and she described herself as "in a daze" as she directed the details of the funeral and the distribution of her mother's possessions.

Bess Wallace Truman brought her mother to live with her in Washington, saying it was a "daughter's duty." Madge Wallace had a well-founded reputation around Independence, Missouri, as a difficult and self-centered woman, but Bess showed the most stoic devotion to her, perhaps out of protective sympathy. At the age of forty-three, Bess's father had taken his own life, leaving Madge with four young children. That suicide, although never discussed during her lifetime, remained the defining event of Bess's life. Eighteen years old at the time, she changed her plans for college in order to stay close to her mother and throughout her life showed Madge boundless attentiveness, even when as First Lady she had many demands on her time.

## Brothers and Sisters

Siblings of presidents and First Ladies have their own place in the nation's history—usually a rather low one and often an embarrassment to the First Family. Presidents' brothers—especially younger brothers—have often appeared misfits and failures, and jokes abound concerning the rewards offered reporters to ignore them. Beer-drinking Billy Carter, who cozied up to the Libyan government, and Roger Clinton, who admitted to a personal history involving drug use, both became embarrassing footnotes to their brothers' administrations.

For presidents' wives, the pattern is a bit more complex. Since she has achieved her position solely by virtue of her marriage, a First Lady's power is considered derived, not personally earned or attained, and she is often caught in a contradictory situation. She risks belittlement for having a free ride, while at the same time she is expected to use her position to help her family. A word to a publisher or a reporter, a ticket to a game or a play, a plane ride or job recommendation—these are all favors that any CEO in the business world expects to pass out. In the White House, the national CEO's wife will be expected to deliver favors too.

If a brother or sister has political ambitions, a boost from a First Lady can help enormously. Eleanor Roosevelt's only brother, Hall, never ran for public office. (Eleanor remarked that although he was very bright, he lacked the ability to compromise that every successful lawmaker needs.) After his death, however, his former wife, Dorothy Kemp Roosevelt, ran for the U.S. House of Representatives from Michigan, and Eleanor campaigned for her. Though Dorothy later lost the general election to a popular Republican, she won the 1942 Democratic primary, the first woman to win statewide in Michigan. As she later admitted, the Roosevelt name probably helped, but Eleanor's endorsement was not insignificant. The First Lady had traveled to Michigan to give a radio talk from her sister-in-law's home. So great was her fame that one of her young nieces managed to turn a profit from the appearance, charging her friends one dollar each to watch Eleanor through the window.

Half a century later, Hillary Rodham Clinton faced the prospect of her brother running for office while she was First Lady. Although he had a job as a public defender in Dade County, Florida, Hugh Rodham appeared to be rather unsettled for a man forty years old. He had never married and admitted that he had not even voted until 1992, when his brother-in-law headed the Democratic national ticket. Proximity to big-

When her brother, Hugh, campaigned for a seat in the U.S. Senate from Florida, First Lady Hillary Rodham Clinton came in to help.

time politics evidently whetted his appetite, and within a year after his sister moved into the White House, Hugh Rodham went on a national television program, *Larry King Live,* to announce his candidacy for U.S. senator from Florida.

The media made much of his relationship with the First Lady. *USA Today* reported that Hugh had ignored his sister's advice not to run against the popular incumbent, and *The Wall Street Journal* printed jokes about "First Brother-in-law." One cartoon implied that Hillary might finally jettison the use of "Rodham" in her name (after insisting on including it throughout Bill's presidential campaign), and some Republicans dismissed Hugh Rodham as "Billy Carter with a law degree."

Hugh Rodham persevered in his uphill campaign in spite of the jests, but not until he had won the primary on his own did his famous sister come in to help. On October 1, 1994, she went to Florida to campaign beside him, and he described their joint appearance as "the crowning achievement" of his life. Unfortunately for him, he was correct: on election day, the voters sent the popular incumbent senator back for another term.

Having a sibling in the White House will transform normally private matters into subjects for public scrutiny and discussion. When Bill Clinton's brother got married in March 1994, reporters asked whether or not he would get a White House ceremony. (He did not.) When Hillary's brother Tony wed a few months later, the same question arose. (He did.)

Even the most innocent actions and associations of her relatives can cause a First Lady embarrassment, and when their behavior verges on the scandalous or unacceptable, she is besieged. Most of Mary Todd Lincoln's large family fought for the Confederacy in the Civil War, and much as she tried to distance herself from them, she could not manage it. False rumors of her disloyalty circulated constantly. When her half-sister's husband was killed in battle at Chattanooga, his widow moved into the White House, leading to more rumors about a "traitorous" First Lady.

Sometimes a president's wife realizes she has little choice but to keep up a brave front and hope people forget quickly. Ida Saxton McKinley (1897–1901) showed the wisdom in this approach when her only brother, George Saxton, was murdered. Forty-year-old George was something of an embarrassment to the Saxton clan, most of whom were respected bankers and solid citizens around Canton, Ohio. His well-developed reputation as a callous ladies' man might have remained within the confines of northern Ohio had not a local dressmaker, whom he had discarded after a long liaison, decided to get even. Her husband had divorced her because of her relationship with George, and she warned him that she would kill him if he did not give up his new love.

On the evening of October 7, 1898, while First Lady Ida McKinley and her sister were greeting guests at an important White House reception, George Saxton rode his bicycle across Canton to call on his latest romantic interest. As he started up the steps of the house, a female figure stepped out of the shrubbery and shot him three times in the stomach, killing him almost instantly. Witnesses identified the dressmaker, and gunpowder residue taken from her hands implicated her in the crime, but she behaved with such dignity throughout her trial that she won over most of the town, including the jury, who found her innocent. Six months later, she walked away a free woman.

Had the victim not been related to the president's family, the murder might never have made national news; but as the brother of the First Lady, George Saxton merited front-page coverage. His death made headlines in the *New York Times,* effectively pushing a crisis in the Philippines to the bottom of the page.

Ida McKinley, who suffered from epilepsy and was considered almost an invalid, had a knack for coming up with sufficient energy in times of emergency, and she appeared to take her brother's murder and the scandal in stride. So inscrutable was her demeanor that some observers questioned if she knew what had happened. After the funeral, she returned immediately to Washington and picked up a heavy social schedule where she had left off, attending a festive White House dinner, inviting friends for cards, and taking part in theater parties. She accom-

Neither Ida McKinley's frail health nor her brother's murder deterred her from an active social schedule.

panied the president on several trips that winter, going once to New York and twice to Atlanta. Through the whole time, she showed no inclination to exchange her expensive, exquisitely made gowns for dowdy mourning dress. Whether it was shrewdness or stoicism, Ida McKinley put her husband's interests above other considerations. If attention to her brother's murder could harm the president, then she would pretend it never happened.

## Wife of a Busy Man

How a First Lady appears to care for her husband is no merely private concern. Voters may question the fitness for high office of anyone whose spouse lacks enthusiasm for the candidate or the office. Americans have never quite approved the idea that a president's wife might refuse to live in the White House or to relinquish her own career, as her counterpart in Italy did in the 1980s. Carla Voltolina, a psychologist married to President Sandro Pertini, continued practicing, used her own name, and declined to ride in official cars or live in the official residence through-out her husband's seven years in office—all without objection from the public. Americans show little sign of permitting a presidential wife such independence.

Eleanor Roosevelt illustrated some latitude in the job of First Lady, traveling thousands of miles on her own rather than staying at home to attend to her husband's comfort. She explained she acted as his mobile eyes and ears: she went because his limited mobility—the result of polio—made traveling painful and difficult for him. Although many Americans accepted her independence, not everyone approved of her being away from home so much. Franklin's mother, who doted on her only child, learned never to assume she knew her daughter-in-law's whereabouts. When informed that she was actually spending a night in the White House, Sara Delano Roosevelt wrote tartly, "I think it's a good thing."

Nancy Reagan frequently said she gladly gave up her acting career to have a happy marriage. *(above)* Sometimes called the "Three Musketeers," the Trumans posed for this photo while Harry Truman was a U.S. senator. *(opposite)*

Visitors to the White House described what often seemed like separate establishments, and Eleanor underscored the gulf between them by writing, in the manner of an employee rather than wife, of waiting for "my regular time to see him." But a large staff looked after Franklin's comfort; their daughter Anna, assorted aides, friends, and relatives supplied him with companionship and fun, and Eleanor went her own way.

More typical White House partnerships involve closer cooperation. Lady Bird Johnson had run a television station and mothered two daughters before becoming First Lady, but she put Lyndon at the top of her list, saying, "I really wanted to serve my husband and serve the country." Rosalynn Carter stressed that she and Jimmy had always been "partners," and she made no secret of how hard she had worked for his success. When he first ran for governor of Georgia in 1966, she became physically ill at the prospect of giving a speech, but a decade later, she was a seasoned "pro" on the campaign trail. Publicity-shy Bess Truman disliked the political life, and when she finally consented to answer reporters' questions about her feelings on the subject, she revealed more than she may have realized. Asked if she had wanted her husband to be president, she replied, "Definitely not," emphasizing "definitely." Yet she stayed the course, through Harry's eighteen years in Washington, and no one recalled hearing her complain.

In no case is wifely devotion better documented than in that of Nancy Reagan. As a Hollywood starlet, she had listed as her ambition in life "to have a successful, happy marriage," and she often declared, "My life began when I met my husband." Nothing in her record suggests she ever deviated from her goal—and her devotion had little to do with the career her husband chose. One wag speculated that if Ronald Reagan had become an automobile salesman, Nancy would have pitched in to dust the interiors of the cars.

More than a century earlier, another president's wife earned her own accolades for wifely devotion. Although Lucy Hayes (1877–1881) had a

An unusual photograph of the Hayes family (because they were almost always pictured with friends and guests) shows Rutherford and Lucy (center, second row) surrounded by their four sons, one daughter-in-law, and daughter (lower right).

large family, her record suggests that Rutherford always came ahead of her children. During one of her visits with him during the Civil War, her two-year-old son died. Although she described it as the "bitterest hour" of her life, she sent the boy's body back to Ohio for burial while she remained with Rutherford. The following year, when she received a telegram that he had been wounded, she left her children, including an infant she had been breast feeding, and went to Washington to find him and supervise his recovery.

In the White House, Lucy's devotion to her husband showed up in small gestures. She disliked domestic duties but performed them with sufficient grace to make him look good. The feminism that she had shown in her youth when she had argued for equal pay for women—an astounding suggestion in the 1850s—had been camouflaged so completely that it may have disappeared by the time she became First Lady. When her female relatives urged her to use her clout in support of woman's suffrage, she refused. When the suffragist leaders Susan B. Anthony and Elizabeth Stanton came calling at the White House, Lucy let them talk with the president alone, and she showed up only to conduct them on a tour of the premises.

This particular side of being First Lady—looking out for the president's health and his success—has been a conspicuous part of the job for two centuries and shows little sign of diminishing. Women as diverse as Lou Hoover and Jacqueline Kennedy have reaffirmed it; Lou referred frequently to making a "background for Bert." Better positioned than vice presidents (who might be suspected of self-promotion) and staff members (who may have their own agendas or lack access), presidential wives play unique roles.

In any description of the job of First Lady, her family role is implied rather than spelled out. Yet it colors her husband's administration and affects her place in history. Pollsters today, focusing on her official tasks, often omit it from their list of important qualities, concentrating on "leadership" and "charisma" instead. But with millions of Americans watching how she gets along with her husband and children, cares for her parents, and deals with her siblings, a smart First Lady will not neglect her family role.

President Kennedy met the First Lady and daughter Caroline upon their return from Europe in 1962.

# "Associate President"

ot long before Nancy Reagan left Washington, a major newspaper concluded that she had

"expanded the role of First Lady into a sort of Associate Presidency." She had helped the chief exec-

utive make major decisions, substituted for him at public events, led her own staff in pursuit of

causes that lent popularity to his administration, and

gone in his place to foreign countries. What the news-

paper failed to note was that Mrs. Reagan had not

On her trip to the South Pacific in 1943, Eleanor Roosevelt greeted many American servicemen and then relayed their messages to their families at home. *(opposite)* Aboard *Air Force One,* Nancy Reagan participated in discussions with the president's staff. *(above)*

Although never elected to any office, Martha Washington realized she could not escape a public role. *(above)* Less than one month after becoming First Lady, Hillary Rodham Clinton met with many legislators, including Senate Majority Leader George J. Mitchell. *(opposite)*

originated that concept of First Ladyship—it had been two centuries in the making.

## Martha Washington Sets Precedents

Almost exactly two hundred years before the Reagans retired to California, Martha Washington (1789–1797) arrived in Manhattan to begin defining how the spouse of a democracy's leader should behave. It was no easy task. Although her husband had just been chosen to lead their new republic, Americans showed signs of wanting a royal personage at his side, and New Yorkers greeted her as though she were a queen. Cannons boomed a thirteen-gun salute, and crowds cheered them all the way to the house Congress had rented for the president on Cherry Street.

Martha had already sampled public life during the American Revolution. Each winter when the family estate at Mt. Vernon required less of her attention, she traveled to wherever the commander in chief happened to be encamped. Although she heard herself applauded as "Lady Washington," much of her day centered on mundane tasks. She assisted with food preparation, visited the sick and wounded, and even did a bit of mending. When admirers came to visit, she received them wearing a "checked apron" and quietly suggested they each try to do more for the cause of independence.

Just how Martha Washington would convert her wartime status remained unclear, and she found little guidance in the Constitution, whose framers had hammered out the office of president from many differing but strongly held opinions. How the chief executive would be elected, how long he would serve, even his title and his social schedule had all been debated at length. This was, after all, an untried experiment to produce a leader more powerful than that the individual states had known since independence, but not so powerful as to alienate the people as the king of England had done.

Had the framers of the Constitution known what lay ahead, they might also have discussed what role the chief executive's family should play; but there is no evidence that the subject ever came up. By leaving so much of the presidency undefined, open to reshaping by whoever held the job, and by permitting the president to choose advisers at will, they set the stage for men to rely heavily on their wives. The first of them, Martha Washington, a matron of fifty-eight, arrived in the temporary capital that spring day in 1789 with only her instincts and good sense to guide her.

## Running the President's Office-Residence

Because the Washingtons decided that the president's residence would double as his office, Martha was drawn into George's work in a way that would not have happened if he had attended to business elsewhere. In the beginning, she held "open house" as visitors of all kinds appeared at all hours of the day. Finally, the president took space in a New York newspaper to announce that he would see social callers only on Tuesday and Friday afternoons between the hours of two and three. Anyone on official business could come at other times—except Sunday, when he wanted to see no one at all.

More than one chief executive would later object to combining office and residence at one location, even one as large and elegant as the White House. Chester Arthur complained that it was like "living above the store," and several presidential wives were just as critical. Louisa Adams (1825–1829) noted that she could hardly be oblivious of the many callers who came each day, even though her husband, John Quincy Adams, showed no interest in her opinions. "I have nothing to do with the disposal of affairs and have never but once been consulted," Louisa wrote. Four decades later, Julia Grant suggested that her family continue living on I Street and use the White House only for work and official entertaining. But the precedent had been set: Americans wanted

their chief executive and his family to reside in the White House.

The Washingtons never actually lived in the President's House in the Federal City—it had not yet been finished when George left office—but Martha oversaw management of the rented houses that served them in the interim. Her large staff, including tavern keeper Sam Fraunces, who had attracted General Washington's attention during the war, helped arrange for food service and other comforts for the many guests who attended the president's receptions on Tuesday afternoons, her parties on Friday evenings, and dinners throughout the week.

## Covering the President's Absence

Outside their home, Martha substituted for George on many occasions, although she did not care for the role. When he did not feel well enough to attend a church service but thought his absence might cause alarm, she went, thus allaying fears that he might be seriously ill. Her trips to

In this 1970 painting by Louis S. Glanzman, Louisa Adams is shown winding silk from silkworms. Though she was shut out of political decisions, Louisa knew that she was watched for some indication of what her husband, John Quincy Adams, was thinking.

**Young Frances Cleveland (center, front) met frequently with wives of cabinet members.**

the circus brought her accolades reserved for public personages, making her feel "like a state prisoner." When George's two presidential terms finally came to an end, she pronounced herself as gleeful as a child released from school.

The custom of having a First Lady stand in for her husband on social or state occasions would later become commonplace, but in 1893, twenty-nine-year-old Frances Cleveland covered for her husband in a different way. Early that summer, at the beginning of Grover Cleveland's second term, doctors found a growth in the top of the president's mouth, and they recommended surgery. But a serious economic down-swing, beginning what would later be described as the worst depression of the century, indicated that this was no time for word to spread that the nation's leader was incapacitated. His young wife played a crucial role in keeping his illness secret.

As the Clevelands prepared for their annual summer vacation at their home in Buzzards' Bay, Massachusetts, they devised a plan to mislead the press. On June 30, they set off from Washington together, but somewhere along the way Grover left the train and boarded a yacht equipped for surgery and staffed like a small hospital. While he underwent surgery, Frances, nearly seven months pregnant, continued on to Massachusetts with their two-year-old daughter, Ruth.

At first, no one remarked on the travel arrangements, but when the president had not yet rejoined his family by July 4, reporters started questioning his whereabouts. Although the surgery had been successful, Grover was in no condition to be seen or to give interviews—bandages still impeded his speaking, and he looked like a very ill man. Given just a little more time to recuperate out of sight, he might be able to conceal the surgery; but if newspapers raised suspicions about his health, the nation could suffer.

Frances acted quickly to dispel rumors and ward off dangerous speculation. She called correspondents to her home and asked them not to print disquieting stories because no mystery surrounded the president—he would arrive shortly. Her pleas evidently worked: the reporters left, and Grover walked into his house that evening without being observed.

Only one article on the surgery appeared at the time, and it was quickly disavowed, its author vilified as "a liar and a faker" (although, in fact, his account was accurate). Grover Cleveland chose never to discuss the incident publicly. He recovered fully and survived another fourteen years, dying of unrelated causes. Not until 1917 did one of the surgeons involved publish a full account of the deception and, in the process,

Edith Galt Wilson insisted she made no decisions for her sick husband—she only selected which papers and people he would see.

underline the very important role the First Lady had taken. Without her cooperation, it is difficult to imagine that the ruse could have worked.

## Guarding Access

By a strange coincidence, the surgeon's article in the *Saturday Evening Post* revealed the truth about Frances Cleveland's role just as Americans were getting to know a particularly forceful First Lady, Edith Galt Wilson (1915–1921), who would later be singled out as one of the most powerful presidential wives in the nation's history. Exactly how powerful she became is debatable, but she remains one of the most hotly discussed of all presidents' wives precisely because she guarded access to her husband during a crucial period in modern history.

A striking forty-three-year-old widow when she met the recently widowed Woodrow Wilson in the spring of 1915, Edith Galt appeared an unlikely match for him. A poorly educated woman, whose writing one historian has described as an "almost illegible scrawl," she had shown no previous interest in politics and even admitted that in the 1912 election, when Woodrow captured the presidency, she could not have named the candidates.

But the attraction between them was apparently immediate, and Woodrow and Edith began spending a great deal of time together. When apart, they exchanged ardent declarations of devotion. Woodrow would have married her very soon, despite advisers' warnings that he risked offending some voters. His first wife, the popular Ellen Wilson, had died in August 1914, and a remarriage less than twelve months later seemed likely to arouse comment. "Better wait," he was told, until after the voters had reelected him in 1916. The enamored chief executive delayed a bit—but only until December 1915. Then he wed Edith Galt at her Washington town house.

For the remaining five years of his presidency, they were nearly inseparable. They sat like young lovers in the White House garden, deciphering war messages. When he had to write a speech, he carried his typewriter up to an office in the residence, where he liked to work, and typed out a first draft while his bride stayed close by. She accompanied him to Paris for the peace talks at the end of World War I, and together they toured Italy and England.

But after Woodrow's collapse in the fall of 1919, Edith took charge of his recovery, and her role changed from doting romantic partner to commanding overseer. When he suffered a stroke while touring the western states, she directed their return to the capital and subsequently monitored his visitors and workload. Every caller went to the president's wife first. Few, other than his doctor, got past her.

Nonpartisan journalists, Republican leaders, and fellow Democrats —none of whom had much experience with women in leadership roles—made much of her power. One magazine reported that the Wilsons' housekeeper had called Edith the "Assistant President," and another publication charged her with coming "close to carrying the burden of First Man." Powerful Senator Henry Cabot Lodge grumbled, "A regency was not contemplated in the Constitution," and Senator Albert Fall accused Edith of "petticoat government" and of upgrading the title of First Lady to "Acting First Man."

Although the president recovered sufficiently to resume control within a few weeks, speculation about Edith's role continued well after her death in 1961. She always insisted that she never "made a single decision regarding the disposition of public affairs," that she was only looking out for her husband's well-being. Historians have generally agreed that she had scant influence on national policies and decisions. Although she may have bolstered Woodrow's resolve to remove Secretary of State Lansing, a man she neither liked nor trusted, this was nothing new: presidents' wives had been nudging their husbands regarding staff and advisers since the beginning of the Republic. Her actions during the nearly forty years she survived Woodrow lend credence to her claim that she

Helen Taft (seated) enlisted her daughter's help with White House entertaining. *(above)* When Helen Taft rode beside her husband to the White House, she made headlines—and set a precedent that her successors would follow. *(opposite)*

remained aloof from politics while she was First Lady. In 1930 when Eleanor Roosevelt approached her for an endorsement of a woman running for office, Edith refused, saying that she cared little about who won.

## Campaigning behind the Scenes

Had she really cared about politics and taking power, Edith Wilson could have learned a lesson from one of her less known predecessors. Helen Herron Taft (1909–1913) had, in fact, played an important part in getting her husband into the executive mansion. She took pride in his success and delighted in referring to the president as "my husband," but William Howard Taft himself showed less enthusiasm for the job. Two different White House servants reported that the first words they heard him utter after his inauguration were, "I'm president now and tired of being kicked around."

Even when Helen and Will Taft were young, her ambition exceeded his, and from the time they met in Cincinnati, Ohio, in the 1880s, she helped shape his career. It was at one of the salons she organized with her sister that she met the Taft brothers, one of them destined to start an important school in Connecticut and the other to serve as president and then chief justice of the Supreme Court. With an uncanny ability to pick the winner, she married the brother who guaranteed her a bigger place in history books.

As a young wife, Helen busied herself with her family while Will worked his way up through several judgeships to take a seat on the U.S. Federal Circuit Court. But larger prizes interested her, and when he was offered the presidency of the Philippines Commission in 1900, she begged him to take it, although she had little idea what it entailed. "It was an invitation from the big world," she later wrote, "and I was willing to accept it at once and investigate its possible complications afterwards." Friends cautioned that moving halfway around the world might be upsetting to her three children, who ranged in age from three to

Lou Hoover reached out to young Americans in many ways—meeting with them, speaking to them on the radio, and urging them to participate in sports.

eleven, but she remained undeterred. She later confessed that the only thing she missed about Cincinnati was the Orchestra Association, which she had helped run.

When President Theodore Roosevelt brought the Tafts back from the Philippines to install Will in his cabinet as secretary of war, Helen bided her time—but when she heard rumors of a possible appointment for her husband to the Supreme Court, she intervened. On a visit to the White House when she was a young girl, she had set her sights on living there, and even Will's clear preference for a judgeship would not divert her. Helen made an appointment with the president, and although she left no record of the meeting, Theodore Roosevelt's few words on the subject are revealing. "After a half hour's talk with your dear wife," he wrote Will Taft, "I understand why an appointment to the court is not desired at this time."

In 1909, Helen finally achieved First Ladyship, and she made sure people noticed. After Will's inauguration at the Capitol, she rode beside him to the White House, although that place had previously been reserved for the outgoing chief executive or some other male dignitary. "Of course there were objections," she later wrote, "but I had my way and in spite of protests took my place at my husband's side."

While she did not actually sit in on cabinet meetings, as Rosalynn Carter would later do, Helen planted herself right outside the door, her ear tilted to the best advantage. In informal situations, Helen Taft liked to stay close to the president's side so she could supply him with forgotten names or needed numbers. Attempts to divert her often failed; she made it known that she did not want to be shunted off with "uninteresting" women to a lunch or some social affair while important discussions went on around her husband.

Helen Taft's role in her husband's election and his administration—like the roles of most First Ladies before 1933—remained largely hidden from the public, which saw presidents' wives only as ceremonial side-

At her one press conference, Mamie Eisenhower stuck to details of her social schedule.

kicks and encouraging partners. Staff and close associates, in positions to assess wives' real impact, had their own reasons for keeping quiet, although they often discussed among themselves the wife's significant role.

Accounts of Florence Harding (1921–1923) agree on her importance to Warren. She had spent considerable time around her husband's newspaper office in Marion, Ohio, and when he got to the United States Senate, she achieved a reputation as "one of the best informed women in the country" (although not, evidently, about Warren's liaisons with other women). When he ran for the presidency in 1920, she helped

An enthusiastic participant in her husband's political career, Florence Harding appeared frequently at his side.

direct the campaign, vetoing, for example, a plan to reply to a rumor about Warren's family and squelching speculations that he wanted to drop out of the race. "We're in," she shouted to his campaign manager, "until hell freezes over!"

But Florence and her immediate successors refused to engage in public, partisan campaigning for their spouses. Even Eleanor Roosevelt, who shattered so many precedents, demurred in the matter of campaigning for Franklin. Although she had stumped for other candidates, she did not think it "appropriate" to speak out for her husband. Her Republican predecessor was just as reticent. When an enthusiastic supporter sent Lou Hoover a box of "Hoover for President" buttons in 1928, she wrote to thank him but explained that she would pass them out to friends because "neither I nor any member of my family would wear one."

The nonpartisan "feminine" face on candidates' wives faded slowly. Even in the 1950s, Mamie Eisenhower limited herself mostly to traveling with Ike, smiling, and waving to crowds. When she published an article in *Good Housekeeping,* she gave it an entirely uncontroversial title: "Vote for my Husband or Vote for Adlai Stevenson, But Please Vote."

## Openly Partisan Campaigning

In the 1960 Kennedy-Nixon campaign, that reticence suddenly became passé. The proliferation of television sets made the candidates (and their families) household names, and wives hesitated to feign a lack of conviction. For the first time in any presidential election, both candidates' wives held college degrees and had worked—Pat Nixon as a teacher and Jacqueline Kennedy as a photographer-reporter. To act as though they had no opinions about the outcome of the race would have made them appear naive, if not actually stupid and unappealing.

Both Pat Nixon and Jacqueline Kennedy got caught up in that race. As one major newspaper reported: "Never before have the wives of both candidates been so active." The Republicans put great stock in Pat's ability to draw votes, and the party's top strategists concluded that "for the first time in American history one woman could conceivably swing a presidential election." The women's division scheduled a "Pat Week" of coffee hours and rallies. News releases from Republican headquarters reminded voters that they were electing a First Lady as well as a president, and that her job "is more than glamour. . . . She represents America to all the world. Pat Nixon is part of the experienced Nixon team. She's uniquely qualified for the position of First Lady."

Jacqueline Kennedy limited her campaigning after July (when she revealed that she was pregnant), but she continued to attract enormous attention. Seventeen years younger than Pat Nixon, she struck voters as coming from a different generation, and her emphasis on elegance and glamour contrasted with Pat's "plain cloth coat" image. Some Americans thought Jackie spent too much on clothes (she joked with reporters about wearing "sable underwear"), but she continued to draw crowds. In New York's El Barrio she spoke in Spanish, and she contributed a column, "Campaign Wife," to the Democratic National Committee newspaper.

The 1960 campaign also brought Lady Bird Johnson out on the campaign stump. As a senator's wife, she had been active in Washington and had even run Lyndon's office when he was away briefly in World War II. But after he consented to join John Kennedy's ticket (against her advice and wishes), she signed up for speech lessons. A novice in the beginning (she later estimated that she had given no more than half a dozen speeches before 1960), she learned quickly and in the course of a few weeks traveled thirty-five thousand miles to speak to voters. Robert Kennedy, John's campaign manager, credited her with moving many votes to the Democratic column.

In 1964, when Lyndon Johnson headed his party's ticket, Lady Bird took on a larger task, one that no candidate's wife had ever attempted

Although her doctors advised against making the trip, a pregnant Jacqueline Kennedy campaigned with her husband in New York City in 1960.

before. Lyndon's civil rights record had alienated many southern voters, and he feared they would vent their anger at the polls, costing him several states. Lady Bird, who insisted that people would respect your stand if you explained why you took it, volunteered to journey through the South and campaign for Lyndon on her own. On the "Lady Bird Special" she steamed out of Washington into the Carolinas and over to New Orleans, giving forty-seven speeches along the way. Advisers, staff, and, for part of the trip, her daughters joined her while the president remained in Washington. More than one observer thought she had changed some minds and helped win a landslide victory for Lyndon in November.

In 1976, Rosalynn Carter further enlarged the role of political spouse by campaigning separately from Jimmy throughout his long presidential race. They could cover double the territory, she pointed out, if they divided it between them. Rosalynn actually started a full eighteen months before the nominating convention, at a time when Jimmy Carter was very much a dark horse, his name little known outside Georgia. Even his own mother had not fully assessed his potential; when he told her he was going to run for president, she asked, "President of what?"

By the 1980s, when an uninvolved First Lady would have been as great an anachronism as a politically active wife a century earlier, Nancy Reagan and Barbara Bush had become adept performers in front of television cameras. Viewers of interview shows heard them denounce the opposition and tout their own spouses.

A few television programs became favorite forums for political statements, and in 1992, Hillary Clinton (1993– ) chose *60 Minutes* to play her crucial role in keeping Bill's candidacy alive. A supermarket tabloid had just run headlines—MY 12-YEAR AFFAIR WITH BILL CLINTON—quoting Gennifer Flowers, a young Arkansas woman. Had the story remained in the *Star,* it might have been ignored; but other media, including such

Well before most women could vote, First Ladies' photos were used on campaign badges. *(above)* Lady Bird Johnson made history when she campaigned on her own for her husband in 1964. *(opposite)*

Hillary Rodham Clinton appeared with her husband on *60 Minutes* in January 1992, to deal with questions about their marriage.

mainstream newspapers as the *New York Times,* picked up the story. When the Clinton campaign could no longer ignore the story, the largest possible audience was selected to counter it: one hundred million viewers who would be sitting in front of their television sets following the Super Bowl on January 26 and would probably stay tuned for *60 Minutes.* Hillary agreed to appear alongside her husband and talk about her marriage, a concession no one recalled any other candidate's wife having made, at least on national television.

Hillary's long experience in public speaking—she had argued court cases and knew how to face a television camera—served her well. As her husband hedged, admitting to "causing pain" in his marriage, she was more forthright, and she left many viewers with the impression that whatever had happened, it was the Clintons' business, not the voters'. Hillary concluded her remarkable performance with a touch of defiance that Bill did not match. She told Americans if they did not like what they saw, "then heck, don't vote for him."

## "Government Official"

After Bill Clinton's victory in November 1992, neither he nor Hillary concealed her role in his administration. When congressional leaders journeyed to Little Rock for a preinauguration conference, her husband openly acknowledged that she had sat in on all the discussions, "talked a lot and knew more than we did about some things." From her wide circle of colleagues and friends, she culled a list of potential nominees for high-level jobs, many of them women. After the inauguration, she took an office in the West Wing, where the president's closest staff work—a first for a president's wife, who usually remained in the East Wing. She then broke all precedent by chairing a huge Task Force on Health Care Reform, responsible for delivering the centerpiece of Bill's campaign promises.

Other First Ladies had lobbied for causes, but none of them

attracted the kind of attention that was focused on Hillary. When Rosalynn Carter testified in favor of the Mental Health Act before a Senate committee in 1979, she spoke from long experience and genuine conviction, but that legislation was hardly the defining element of Jimmy's administration. Eleanor Roosevelt's appearance before a congressional committee in 1942 did not even merit a mention in most newspapers.

Hillary Rodham Clinton's high-profile job involved considerable political risk, but she showed little evidence of calculating the possible fallout. If her commission failed to deliver, she risked embarrassing the president, who could hardly distance himself from a wife or fire her, as he might with an unpopular staffer or cabinet member. On the other hand, if the commission produced a comprehensive plan, it would likely meet opposition from many quarters for a variety of reasons. Health care swallowed a huge chunk of the nation's budget, and any change in how the system worked would affect almost everyone.

Inadvertently, Hillary's chairmanship of the task force led to a legal ruling on the role of First Ladies. Physicians and other health care professionals sought to participate in the task force discussions but were barred under a rule that permitted closed meetings of "government officials." The doctors went to court and argued that the First Lady was neither a government official nor, as her attorneys had argued, "the functional equivalent," and that the meetings should therefore be open to anyone who wanted to attend.

A district federal judge concurred with the physicians, but on appeal that decision was reversed. The appeals court accepted the argument that a long tradition "of public service by First Ladies" entitled them to the "government official" designation. They have acted, said the majority decision, "as advisers and personal representatives of their husbands." Even a dissenting opinion underlined the considerable privileges a First Lady enjoys: she is "greeted like a head of state, guarded by the Secret

Rosalynn Carter met with the president, vice president, and top advisers before embarking on her trip to the Caribbean and South America in 1977.

Service and allowed to spend Federal money." Because the task force had already concluded its deliberations and disbanded, the court's decision had little practical effect, except to reaffirm the acceptance of official status for the president's spouse.

## Heading a Cause of Her Own

Hillary Rodham Clinton put her efforts into the president's agenda, and when the health care program floundered, she suffered the consequences, but most of her predecessors had staked out their own projects, usually nonpolitical. Lady Bird Johnson, who realized that Jacqueline Kennedy's White House restoration lent luster to Camelot, understood the wisdom of distancing herself from the Oval Office. Her decision to focus on the environment and highway beautification was motivated partly by the knowledge that Lyndon would stay out of it. She wanted a cause she cared about, "something that makes the heart sing," she said, one that complemented Lyndon's "Great Society" programs but was her own. Rosalynn Carter also showed the value of claiming her own turf when she focused on mental health care reform, related to Jimmy's objectives but distinctively her own.

The association of presidents' wives with causes of their own goes back at least to Woodrow Wilson's first wife, Ellen Axson Wilson (1913–1914). A spirited and independent woman in her youth, Ellen left tiny Rome, Georgia, to study painting in New York City. Living in a boarding house in Greenwich Village, she had to fend for herself. Her parents had both died, and her budget did not permit a chaperone or companion, but she formed a network of friends at the Art Students' League and at the "missionary school" where she taught two evenings each week. By the time she moved into the White House, she had little time for painting, although she set aside one room in the mansion for her easel.

Her social conscience had survived, and she concentrated on improving housing. In Washington's poor neighborhoods, just a few

blocks from the Oval Office, dilapidated buildings and alley slums were common, and Ellen decided to show oblivious legislators what could be done to improve them. She invited congressmen and senators for tea, introduced them to housing reformers, and arranged for cars to take them on tours of blighted areas. The topic of slum clearance attained such vogue that one insider insisted it was impossible to move in polite society without a full knowledge of it.

Ellen Wilson became ill with a kidney disease and died in August 1914, before she could get much changed. But as she lay dying, the United States Senate acknowledged her efforts by passing "Mrs. Wilson's Alley Bill." The House of Representatives quickly followed suit, marking an unprecedented linking of a First Lady's name to legislation.

Noncontroversial causes worked best (few people had the heart to

Beautification went beyond planting flowers for Lady Bird Johnson—it included drawing the entire community into helping.

In her work with the Girl Scouts, Lou Hoover emphasized the importance of athletics as well as domestic skills. *(above)* **Nancy Reagan's "Just Say No" campaign reached out to schoolchildren.** *(opposite)*

defend slums, much as they hated the idea of paying to raze them), and several of Ellen Wilson's successors found equally popular projects. Lou Hoover gave her nod to the Girl Scouts and to women's athletics in general. Florence Harding boosted the Red Cross; Mamie Eisenhower and Bess Truman added the March of Dimes to their list of First Lady causes.

Nancy Reagan (1981–1989) had first supported the Foster Grandparents Program while Ronald was governor of California, and she took that cause with her to the White House. But somehow it did not sell. The idea of Nancy Reagan, whose well-groomed chic did not seem grandmotherly, leading a program that matched senior citizens with ghetto youth did not resonate with many Americans. Other problems beset her during her first year in Washington. The assassination attempt on the president in March 1981 frightened and shocked her; sharp media criticism of what some people considered excessive spending on clothes and new White House china dismayed her.

Still, Nancy remained determined to do what she could for her husband's administration, and if her low popularity ratings pulled down his, she would change. In a meeting called to work out a plan, advisers urged her to spearhead an antidrug campaign, later labeled "Just Say No." Nancy insisted she had long wanted to join the fight against drug abuse but had been warned away by staffers who thought it too negative and depressing. Her subsequent approval ratings showed how wrong they were. In just a few months she gained twenty points in public opinion polls. Soon she had a staff of several dozen; the project had grown beyond what one person and a group of willing volunteers could handle.

Barbara Bush (1989–1993) continued the tradition of pursuing a cause vigorously. She had zeroed in on literacy about the same time that George began campaigning seriously for the White House, and although he liked to bill himself as the "education president," it was his wife who

Barbara Bush found the motivation for her literacy drive in her own large family.

became most closely associated with the subject in the public's eyes. Barbara argued that illiteracy figured in a great many problems of all kinds and caused a multitude of failures. She had become aware of the importance of reading when she struggled with her own son's dyslexia, and she understood that many parents, burdened with full-time jobs, needed help from outside their families to tutor their youngsters. If improved literacy rates could diminish homelessness, unemployment, and boredom, then Barbara Bush knew where she wanted to concentrate the clout of First Ladyship.

Soon after George's inauguration, she announced the formation of the Barbara Bush Foundation for Literacy, and when she published an amusing photo book about living in the White House, ostensibly written by the family dog, Millie, she donated all the proceeds to the foundation. It was a considerable stake—the book earned nearly $800,000 in royalties, and had she not given the money away, Barbara would have banked far more than George that year.

## *Widening the President's Appeal*

Whether they like it or not, presidential spouses are pushed into an advocacy role by Americans who turn to them for help. The tradition that assumes that the president is too busy to listen but his wife has time extends back more than a century to Lucy Hayes. Her husband's presidency coincided with the mushrooming of the Women's Christian Temperance Union (WCTU), which was founded in 1874 and quickly became the largest women's organization in the nation. WCTU leaders begged Lucy to use her prominence as First Lady to help them convert the nation to teetotaling.

Lucy's biographer later concluded that although she appeased temperance advocates, she did not herself hold strong views on what other people drank. An abstainer herself, she permitted no alcohol at the White House (after an initial dinner at which she served wine and drew a public cry of protest), and she suffered the indignity of hearing herself referred to as "Lemonade Lucy." But she never joined the WCTU

At her first press conference, Betty Ford admitted that she and the president held different opinions on some topics.

Abigail Fillmore, who had been her husband's teacher in school, maintained a scholarly, detached presence in the White House.

(although she joined other organizations), and at the Hayes Presidential Center in Fremont, Ohio, her association with temperance merits scant mention. That she acted wisely is clear from her husband's diary. Just before leaving office, Rutherford Hayes noted that his wife's popularity had helped bring many votes into the Republican column.

Other presidential wives appealed to voters who liked the husbands less. Betty Ford's popularity ran higher in some quarters than Gerald's, partly because she admitted candidly that she differed with him on important issues. At her first news conference, less than a week after she became First Lady, she surprised reporters by describing her own views on abortion as much closer to those of Jacob Javits, the pro-choice New York senator, than to Gerald Ford's. She had previously referred to splitting her ticket in the voting booth—something party regulars discourage. Rather than harming her husband, she attracted her own following, and when he ran (unsuccessfully) for reelection in 1976, campaign buttons plugged "Betty's Husband for President."

But sentiment can also run against an outspoken First Lady, as Eleanor Roosevelt learned. Though more than one liberal admitted to voting for Franklin Roosevelt because of his wife, there were others who reserved their deepest contempt for her. She apparently never considered running for office herself, content to remain an important extension of her husband's administration, but campaigners invoked her name anyway. Opponents printed buttons in 1940 reading "We Don't Want Eleanor either."

Sometimes the First Lady functions as an adjunct to the president—not so much in evidence herself as quietly helping define the impression that he makes. John Eisenhower concluded that his mother, Mamie, had helped smooth out some of the "rough corners" in the Kansas farm boy she had married.

Nearly a hundred years earlier, Abigail Fillmore (1850–1853) lent an intellectual cast to Millard's reputation. She had been his teacher in school, and after their marriage she held salons and invited the outstanding minds of Buffalo to discuss the topics of the day and examine her book collection. As he rose from one political office to another, he relied on her to keep well-informed, and one of their friends concluded that he "never took an important step without her advice and counsel." When they got to the White House and she found that it had no library, she started one on the second floor—her favorite part of the mansion—where she could read and study languages while avoiding the capital's social life.

## Ceremonial Appearances

Presidents' wives too reticent or uncommitted to engage in controversy can make ceremonial appearances to help their husbands. Among the multitude of requests that a chief executive receives—to dedicate new buildings, receive honorary degrees, and lend support to a cause—he can accept only a few. Although they require time, these are lightweight assignments, requiring no speaking of substance. Just showing a face will do, and even the shyest relative can pinch-hit.

Bess Truman (1945–1953), who loathed a public role for herself, went out grudgingly on such chores. She never thrived in the spotlight, and the larger the crowd, the greater her discomfort. Servants reported that her hands perspired profusely at White House receptions. Nevertheless, she agreed to christen two hospital planes in May 1945, just a few weeks after she had become First Lady and before she had fully settled into the job. It seemed a simple task for Bess, who had been an outstanding tennis player in her youth. She stepped forward to swing the champagne bottle against the first plane.

Unfortunately no one had scored the glass first, and it required nine strikes by Bess and four by a military aide before it broke. The First Lady kept her poise as she moved on to the second plane, but this time the bottle had been overprepared, and on the first try, it splattered her and

Bess Truman (holding bottle) disliked public appearances, especially when things went wrong, as on this occasion, when the champagne bottle would not break.

Rosalynn Carter was invited to the Camp David meeting, along with the wives of Anwar al-Sadat (left) and Menachem Begin.

all the other dignitaries around her. Bess was embarrassed, and Harry hardly helped matters. When he jokingly inquired where her celebrated tennis arm had gone, she retorted she would have liked to break the bottle over his head. He suggested quietly to reporters that they would be doing him a large favor if they kept the story to themselves rather than relaying it to the nation, but it proved too humorous to resist and made the major newspapers.

With more success (although not much more enthusiasm), Rosalynn Carter filled in for Jimmy in September 1978. The peace talks at Camp David had gone on far longer than anticipated. President Carter did not wish to leave the meetings with Egyptian President Anwar al-Sadat and Israeli Prime Minister Menachem Begin, but he also did not want to offend Italian American and Hispanic community leaders whom he had agreed to meet. "One of us had to be there," Rosalynn explained, "and it was obviously going to be me," so she helicoptered back to Washington and stood in for the president.

## Receiving Gifts

Of all the substituting that a First Lady does, one of the more pleasant tasks is receiving gifts for the president, and from the very beginning, she has taken offerings that he considered inappropriate to accept himself. George Washington, who loved fine horses, hesitated to take a carriage offered him by the state of Pennsylvania. But Martha could, he decided, and she did.

In 1929, when an admirer sent a shiny new Cadillac to First Lady Lou Hoover, the rules about what gifts presidents and their families could accept had not been fully developed. Lou wrote a graceful note, pointing out that she and her husband generally refused "the many commercial gifts so kindly offered us." But then, the sportswoman who knew and appreciated horses continued, the automobile appealed to her so much, seeming "almost like a new colt come in from the pasture," that she could not resist adding it to her "Cadillac stable."

In the early years, First Ladies saw nothing wrong with accepting gifts intended, no doubt, to make a favorable impression on the president, but by the mid-nineteenth century this had already come into question. Harriet Lane, James Buchanan's young niece, who served as her bachelor uncle's popular White House hostess (1857–1861), was pleased that many newborn girls had been named for her and a song dedicated to her, but she found it hard to resist more tangible tributes. When a young man proffered a diamond bracelet, she hesitated—she had already been criticized for keeping some valuable pictures, and she feared her uncle would frown on costly jewelry. Finding him in a particularly good mood one day, she asked if she could keep some pebbles

Her youth helped make Harriet Lane an extremely popular White House hostess for her bachelor uncle, James Buchanan.

sent by an admirer. The president assured her no one would object to an insignificant gift, and she gleefully accepted the bracelet, explaining to friends, "Diamonds are pebbles, you know."

## Representing the President Abroad

By the 1960s, expensive gifts were frowned on, but Jacqueline Kennedy won admirers at home and abroad who would have cheerfully deluged her with presents. On the first European trip the Kennedys took after his inauguration, she won over most of the French, who had rarely encountered a foreign leader's wife who spoke their language faultlessly, understood their culture, and dressed like a fashion model. The enthusiastic reception led a proud American president to quip: "I would like to introduce myself. I am the man who accompanied Jacqueline Kennedy to Paris."

Eleanor Roosevelt demonstrated how successfully a less glamorous First Lady could travel in her husband's place. Her journey to the South Pacific in the autumn of 1943 was a first for a president's wife, and she had her own personal reasons for wanting to make the twenty-thousand-mile trip. Her young friend, Joseph Lash, was stationed at Guadalcanal, although when she set out she had no assurance she would be able to see him. Military brass bristled at the very idea that she insisted on entering a battle area; they worried that they could not guarantee her safety.

In the end, Eleanor spent a few hours with Lash, but it was the enthusiastic reception she got from thousands of soldiers unknown to her that remained her strongest memory. At first she had been nonplussed to be greeted by her first name, as in "Here's Eleanor!" but she decided to take it as a compliment and respond with a cheerful wave. When the men asked her to convey messages to their loved ones back home, she began taking down names. More than one family was surprised to receive a telephone call from the White House, bringing per-

Nancy Reagan showed her country's concern when she toured Mexico City following its devastating earthquake. *(above)* On her South Pacific trip, Eleanor Roosevelt greeted many people, including this Maori woman. *(opposite)*

During her "solo" trip to several countries in western Africa in 1972, Pat Nixon posed in local costume.

sonal greetings from a soldier son or husband.

As wife of the American head of state, Eleanor received a welcome usually reserved for royalty, and several of her successors learned to substitute for their husbands at events involving kings and queens. In March 1964, Lady Bird Johnson flew to Athens for the funeral of King Paul of Greece. Former president Harry Truman shared with her the honor of heading the American delegation, and the two found much to talk about: their southern roots, his ideas on the Marshall Plan, and how he kept busy after leaving the White House. Even though she conversed with dozens of ruling monarchs (plus a few who were "out of work"), it was her time with the eighty-year-old retiree from Missouri that provided what she later called "one of the big pluses of this period of my life." His insight into history awed her.

In addition to these ceremonial trips abroad, First Ladies occasionally make forays into policy matters, although not always successfully, as Rosalynn Carter learned in the spring of 1977. Soon after Jimmy took office, she agreed to visit seven nations in the Caribbean and South America and talk with their leaders about problems facing them and the United States. She brushed up on her Spanish and was briefed by the State Department and the Council of Economic Advisers. Then she set out for what the White House called "substantive" discussions.

When the First Lady returned two weeks later and reported to the Senate Foreign Relations Committee, she found her trip widely criticized. *Newsweek* magazine's Meg Greenfield and others questioned the wisdom of sending a presidential representative who was neither appointed nor elected. To whom was she "accountable," Greenfield queried. Although both Carters defended the venture, Rosalynn never embarked on a similar trip again, explaining that Jimmy was "able to go himself." Instead, she limited herself to goodwill missions more in line with the ceremonial trips of her predecessors, as when she went to Southeast Asia to highlight the problems of refugees or accompanied Jimmy to an economic summit in Venice.

In 1979, Rosalynn Carter traveled to Thailand to show her concern for Cambodian refugees.

## Elizabeth Monroe's Rescue Mission

Although twentieth-century First Ladies traveled thousands of miles to represent the United States government abroad, none undertook quite so risky a mission as did Elizabeth Monroe, when she took a short carriage ride in Paris in 1794. Her adventure predated her husband's presidency by more than two decades, but it lent luster to her name until the day she died.

Elizabeth accomplished her remarkable feat soon after arriving in Paris, where her husband served as minister from the United States. It was the first of what would turn into several diplomatic assignments for the Monroes in Europe, but it was surely the most confusing. Paris was in a state of chaos as factions in the Revolution shifted continually, turn-

Parisians referred to the striking Elizabeth Monroe as *la belle Américaine.*

ing friends into foes overnight. In one of the swings, America's old friend, Marquise de Lafayette, had been imprisoned outside the city and his wife put behind bars in Paris. Mme. Lafayette had every reason to fear for own her life: during a six-week period, 1,500 prisoners, including her mother and other relatives, had been sent to the guillotine.

Much as the Monroes wanted to help the Lafayettes, they understood that they would make matters worse if they acted like foreign meddlers. They decided to try a subtle tack to arouse public sentiment for Mme. Lafayette, then hope that Parisians would pressure the revolutionary leaders to set her free. Elizabeth Monroe, who was not yet known to many French people but was a strikingly beautiful young woman, agreed to ride alone to the prison. Her carriage, deliberately painted to attract attention, drew crowds demanding to know who she was and where she was going. When she arrived at the prison gates, she requested that Mme. Lafayette be brought out, and in full view of the crowd, the two women embraced and chatted. Affected by her gesture, Parisians pressured their leaders to release Mme. Lafayette, and within days she was free.

## Mending Political Fences at Home

Elizabeth Monroe's popularity abroad did her little good in Washington, especially since her predecessor in the White House, Dolley Madison, had emphasized more democratic "mixings" with the people. Among the most charming of all presidents' wives, Dolley had her work cut out for her when she married the intellectual but not very outgoing James Madison. A widow with a young son when she met James, Dorothea Payne Todd—known to all as Dolley—made what historians would later judge a curious but remarkably happy match. Several inches taller than the five-foot-four-inch president, whom she always called "Mr. Madison," she left little doubt about her devotion to him.

On more than one occasion Dolley used her charm to win him

political support. When he fired a secretary of state, Robert Smith, she gave a dinner in the man's honor, and when Smith failed to appear, she went calling on his family "with professions of great affection." In 1812, when James's chances for reelection looked slim, she cheerfully socialized with his opponents as well as his friends and prevailed on those who had at first refused to dine with the president to come "in a large body." Historians later concluded that she deserved at least part of the credit for James's victory that November.

Dolley Madison also initiated the custom—which her successors loathed—of calling on the wives of all legislators who came to live in Washington. Her tenure coincided with new interest in the federal capital, and many members of Congress brought their wives and daughters with them—all eager for a visit from the president's wife. Dolley understood that she could not slight anyone without risk of hurting her husband politically, so she dedicated six days a week to rumbling around the city's still unpaved streets and visiting dozens of houses.

Dolley's successor, Elizabeth Monroe, pleaded poor health and avoided the visits, but Louisa Adams did not have the luxury of refusing. While John Quincy Adams served as secretary of state, he already had his eyes firmly on the White House, and he enlisted Louisa's help in getting there. Each morning, he prepared "as carefully as a commercial treaty" a list of homes for her to visit. "It is understood," she wrote with sarcasm in her diary, "that a man who is ambitious to become president of the United States must make his wife visit the Ladies of the members of Congress first. Otherwise he is totally inefficient to fill so high an office." Sometimes Louisa had to make as many as twenty-five stops in a single day, and she hated every one. "These visits have made me sick many times," she wrote in her diary, "and I really sometimes think they will make me crazy."

The custom of calling fell out of fashion about the time of World War I, and several women, including Lou Hoover and Eleanor

Dolley Madison's expensive turbans, which she sometimes ordered from Paris, caused little controversy because she was so popular.

**When Gerald Ford's campaigning cost him his voice, he turned to his wife to deliver the concession speech.**

Roosevelt, later took credit for changing the social rules. Instead of First Ladies going around town, more people were invited to 1600 Pennsylvania Avenue for a party or a photo, and a president's wife could play "Welcome Wagon" to dozens at a time. Rosalynn Carter developed her own abbreviation—"BOEs"—for the many trips she took from the family quarters on the second floor of the White House to the "Bottom of the Elevator" to pose with various delegations that had come to Washington.

## Advising the President

These ceremonial appearances serve as public reminder of more substantive work First Ladies do behind the scenes. Although difficult to document precisely because it occurs in private, the impact of presidents' wives on public policy extends back to the eighteenth century. When

John Adams made an unpopular appointment, his critics blamed it on Abigail's absence. She had been recuperating in Massachusetts when John wrote her that he had heard grumbling that "had she been here" the error would have been avoided. Knowing that would please her, he added, "This ought to gratify your vanity enough to cure you."

A long parade of influential First Ladies join Abigail, and not all of them have been acknowledged. Sarah Polk (1845–1849) read many newspapers, marking the items that the president needed to see. Even the relatively unschooled Eliza Johnson (1865–1869) clipped articles for Andrew to look at, shrewdly separating the good news, which she gave him in the evening, from the bad, which he got the next morning. Her biographer concluded that Andrew Johnson gave greater weight to the opinions of his wife and daughters than to "any fellow statesman." Gerald Ford admitted discussing with Betty important decisions, including the controversial one to pardon Richard Nixon. For her part, she acknowledged that she used "pillow talk" to relay her views on important issues. Jimmy Carter stressed that he and Rosalynn had always been partners, and he made it clear that he continued to rely on her advice in the White House.

In the case of Bess and Harry Truman, the record is unclear. He told a reporter that Bess shared the burdens of the office, including decisions on the atomic bomb, the Marshall Plan, and Korea. "I discussed all of them with her," he said. "Why not? Her judgment was always good." But their daughter later gave a somewhat different account: she remembered her mother feeling shut out of important deliberations in the White House. The Trumans corresponded frequently whenever they were apart, but the letters that would document exactly what they discussed are missing because Bess destroyed them—against Harry's objections. When he found her burning their correspondence, he urged her to stop and "think of history," but she replied, "I have," and kept burning.

Nancy Reagan's influence on her husband is better documented because it was widely reported on by friends and foes during their eight years in the White House. While the president convalesced from cancer surgery in 1985, observers pointed to a triumvirate in charge—the patient, his chief of staff, and the First Lady. CBS's Dan Rather based his prediction of a successful arms limitation agreement on the fact that "both the president and Mrs. Reagan want an agreement." The *New York Times* noted that when the president of the Philippines and his wife considered fleeing into exile, President Marcos sought advice from Senator Paul Laxalt, a close political associate of Ronald Reagan, but Imelda called Nancy. On one occasion, television cameras caught Nancy suggesting words to the president as he groped for a noncommittal answer to a reporter's question on a sensitive issue. He accepted her prompting, saying "We're doing all we can."

Ronald Reagan publicly acknowledged his devotion to Nancy as well as her impact on policy when he went on radio following one of his operations and talked about the important role of First Ladies: "They aren't elected," he told the nation, "and they don't receive a salary, but in my book they've all been heroes. Abigail Adams helped invent America, Dolley Madison helped protect it. Eleanor Roosevelt was F.D.R.'s eyes and ears." Then he paid special tribute to Nancy, who was, he said, "my everything. When I look back on these days, Nancy, I'll remember your radiance and your strength, your support, and for taking part in the business of the nation. I say for myself, but also on behalf of the nation, 'Thank you, partner. Thanks for everything.'"

In less sentimental tones, many White House sources pointed to Nancy's considerable influence, and some described her as "indispensable" and a "savvy adviser" on matters pertaining to the Soviet Union and on who got hired and fired. In a game of musical chairs involving cabinet members, fingers pointed to Nancy as playing the tune. In his book, *For the Record,* former chief of staff Donald Regan reported that

On "whistle-stop" tours, Harry Truman introduced Bess as "the boss."

Nancy vetoed dates for the president's trips and news conferences, and that she did so following consultations with her California astrologist. The First Lady had insisted on keeping the president convalescing too long after surgery, Regan complained, and the delay had hurt him. "Mrs. Reagan's concern for her husband's health was understandable, even admirable," Regan wrote, "but it seemed to me excessive, particularly since the president himself did not seem to think that there was any need for him to slow down to the point where he was lying dead in the water."

In her own book, *My Turn,* Nancy admitted to wielding some influence over the Oval Office: "For eight years I was sleeping with the president, and if that doesn't give you special access, I don't know what does." But, she declared her influence had been exaggerated: "Believe me, if I really were the dragon lady that [Donald Regan] described in his book, he would have been out the door many months earlier."

Eleanor Roosevelt, also harshly attacked, frequently painted a complicated picture of her role in Franklin's administration. She often insisted that she merely informed the president of what she had seen or heard. "I wouldn't dream of doing more than passing along requests or suggestions that come to me," she wrote. When a man publicly thanked her for finding him a job, she told him that he had put her in "a very embarrassing position" by making it look as though she had influence.

At the same time, however, Eleanor privately acknowledged her impact. Jerre Mangione, who worked with the Federal Writers' Project during the 1930s, remembered a breakfast with the First Lady. Eleanor had begun by revealing how she had disagreed strongly with the president on a matter and then, the next day, she had heard him present her opinion to the British ambassador as though it were his own. "I was so astonished," she told Mangione, "that I almost dropped the teapot."

Tangible results of Eleanor's influence showed up in various laws and policies, although in the beginning, she had to take hints from

Eleanor Roosevelt's attention to the civil rights of all Americans made her popular with many African Americans.

Franklin about how to sleuth. He encouraged her to be suspicious and ask questions. When she visited a school, she learned to peek into the pots and pans to see what schoolchildren were really eating for lunch rather than just accept a printed menu.

Eleanor's own genuine interest in people made her a good detective, and she had a knack for describing what she had seen. On one visit to a poor family in Appalachia, she met a young boy who proudly showed her his pet rabbit. The boy's sister told the First Lady, "He thinks we're not going to eat that rabbit, but he's wrong," causing the boy to clutch his pet and run out of sight. When Eleanor later recounted the story at a White House dinner, one of the guests sent a check "to help keep the rabbit alive."

Much of Eleanor Roosevelt's power resulted from putting the right people together. Molly Dewson, chair of the Women's Division of the

Edith Roosevelt won many accolades as First Lady, and it was sometimes said that she "never made a mistake."

Democratic National Committee, recalled that whenever she wanted to reach Franklin, she simply contacted Eleanor, who invited her to sit next to him at dinner. "The matter was settled," Dewson wrote, "before we finished our soup."

Eleanor Roosevelt was no stranger to the idea of wives and sisters influencing powerful men. Her uncle Theodore had consulted with his sister, Eleanor wrote, and rarely made a decision unless he talked it over with her first. Theodore's wife, Edith, whose tastes ran more to literature than politics, did not hesitate to step in when she thought her judgment was needed. When, after leaving office, Theodore decided to make a long journey to Africa and Europe, he fancied wearing a military uniform, emphasizing the heroic role he had played with his "Rough Riders" in Cuba in 1898. His wife, who realized that he risked ridicule in that attire, persuaded him to scrap the idea. After he returned, sized up the Republican record under his successor William Howard Taft, and found it lacking, Theodore determined to regain the presidency; he ran on a third party ticket in 1912. This time he had chosen to ignore Edith's accurate prediction: "You will never be president again."

## A First Lady's Office

Edith Roosevelt (1901–1909) often receives credit for institutionalizing the First Lady's office because she borrowed Isabella Hagner from the War Department to assist her in White House work. From a desk on the second floor of the executive mansion, Hagner handled correspondence, supplied reporters with details of the president's social schedule, and occasionally fielded questions about the Roosevelt children. By the end of the twentieth century, that one-person operation had grown to a staff of dozens, although most presidents' wives continued to rely heavily on volunteers and friends. In 1953, the *Congressional Directory* made a tiny concession to changes in First Ladyship when it listed Mary McCaffree "Acting Secretary to the president's wife."

In 1961, Jacqueline Kennedy helped cement the idea that the First Lady needed a separate staff when she named her own press secretary, twenty-three-year-old Pamela Turnure. After that, the East Wing staff mushroomed. Lady Bird Johnson's records list more than two dozen full-timers, but the numbers mean little since many more additional specialists came "on loan" from various agencies and departments to work on Lady Bird's beautification project. Her successors continued the practice of borrowing staff from other offices.

Edith Galt Wilson (third from left) accompanied her husband to Europe for the peace talks in 1919 and participated in many of the banquets.

...........................................................

Typically modest in describing their influence, First Ladies have left much of their work undocumented. Historians, attempting to assess the record, have concluded that many played important roles. Abigail Adams was dubbed "Mrs. President." Sarah Polk was "increasingly indispensable" to her husband as "secretary, political counselor, nurse, and emotional resource." Eleanor Roosevelt helped shape the New Deal. Hillary Rodham Clinton was credited (and blamed) for acting as "co-president." No one woman defined the role for all time; dozens contributed to what it could mean.

# Keeper of the White House

**A**mong the most famous homes in the world, the White House is a relatively modest structure whose residents enjoy the prominence of any king or queen. In its early years, it was sometimes referred to as the President's Palace, thus underlining a parallel between the First Lady's role and that of a royal consort. Anthropologist Margaret Mead concluded: "Kings and queens have always focused people's feelings and since we're not very far from a

For the state visit of Queen Elizabeth II and the Duke of Edinburgh in May 1991, Barbara Bush planned a "royal White House evening." *(opposite)* In April 1962, when the Kennedys honored the Shah of Iran at a state dinner, Empress Farah wore remarkable jewelry. *(above)*

Dolley Madison's success as White House hostess encouraged many of her successors to imitate her.

monarchy, the president's wife, whoever she is, has little choice but to serve as our queen."

The regal position of the president's wife became particularly obvious in the early 1960s, when two photogenic young American women made headlines around the world. The First Lady of the United States and Princess Grace of Monaco both became enormously popular, and more than one observer noted a similarity in their roles.

In the details of their lives, Jacqueline Bouvier Kennedy and Grace Kelly were remarkably alike. Born within six months of each other to wealthy Catholic families, they grew up on the East Coast and then took glamorous jobs—one as "inquiring photographer" with a Washington newspaper and the other as a Hollywood actress. Fairy-tale romances culminated in picture-book weddings. They both married prominent men—one, a Massachusetts senator whose eyes were focused firmly on the White House, and the other, a prince whose family had ruled a tiny Riviera principality for nearly seven hundred years. Both women remained public figures until their relatively premature deaths, and each made a permanent addition to the fashion lexicon: the "Jackie" pillbox and the "Kelly" handbag.

The two women faced similar official duties. Standing guard at their respective palaces, each linked her name and tastes to it in a special way. Besides overseeing management of homes boasting more than one hundred rooms, they planned dramatic parties for foreign visitors, and they promoted a variety of charitable causes, often using the "palace" as backdrop. In Mead's terms, they "gladdened the eye" and awakened people "to their cultural heritage."

## Nation's Chief Hostess

High on a First Lady's list of duties is acting as her country's official hostess. She represents an entire nation when she welcomes fellow citizens and foreign visitors to the White House. Dolley Madison (1809–1817)

revealed a few of the risks in this task, and her successors would grapple with others. Dolley had actually apprenticed in the role—before her husband took the oath of office—by agreeing to assist widower Thomas Jefferson, her Virginia neighbor, during his two terms (1801–1809). Throughout her remarkably long tenure, she was both praised and ridiculed for her style, with some observers finding that she bent too low to include everyone and others just as firm in fearing that she was too selective.

Dolley's dinners caused comment, especially from foreigners. Rather than serving many courses in succession, the accepted procedure in Europe, she instructed her servants to put several platters on the table at the same time. The British minister to Washington, Anthony Merry, and

The Kennedys entertained Prince Rainier and Princess Grace of Monaco only once at the White House—for lunch.

Mary Lincoln's parties, held while the nation was divided in a bitter civil war, angered her critics.

his wife likened the result to a "harvest table" for farmers rather than an elegant state dinner for diplomats; but Dolley stuck with her plan and one-upped the Britons by reminding them that she was pleased to live in a country "of plenty" that permitted such abundance.

The ice-cream desserts that Dolley served earned her a permanent place in the nation's history books (although evidence suggests that she may have learned about the frozen delicacy from Thomas Jefferson, who had first tried it in Paris), and her successors sought to make their parties just as special. Like Dolley, each First Lady found her individual taste linked to the White House, and often she was criticized for it. If she stressed elegance, she risked criticism for aping royalty. If she tried to economize, she invited charges that she made an entire nation look bad.

Jacqueline Kennedy quickly took a seat in the elitist camp, saying she wanted to make the president's parties, like everything else about the Kennedy White House, "the best." She varied the themes, the entertainment, and even, on one occasion, the locale when she had guests transported by boat to George Washington's home, Mt. Vernon, for a state dinner. Other Kennedy innovations stressed informality: the hosts mingled with guests rather than standing in stiff receiving lines, and small tables for ten replaced the banquet hall formations favored by previous First Ladies.

History offers several examples of high spenders at 1600 Pennsylvania Avenue—something about the address seemed to pull on the purse. Though later she was sharply criticized, Mary Lincoln, a notorious spendthrift, at first won accolades for her "exquisite taste." In spite of the fact that a bloody civil war divided the nation, *Leslie's Magazine* compared her household to palaces abroad and concluded that Mrs. Lincoln was "second in no respect" to the monarchs of Europe. In stylish low-cut gowns displaying the "exquisitely molded shoulders and arms of our fair 'Republican Queen,'" she was, the periodical boasted, "absolutely dazzling."

Mary Lincoln's lavish spending may well have resulted partly from her own insecurities, but there were other reasons for Julia Grant's expenditures. Confident and self-assured about most things, Julia liked to have a good time, and she proceeded to do so in spite of some nasty press coverage. She had the distinctly bad luck to become First Lady just as women's magazines began to cover the White House in greater detail, and *Godey's Lady's Book* introduced a monthly column on the subject.

Starting in 1873, early in the second Grant administration, reporter Harriet Hazelton relayed the social trivia of the capital as observed by "Aunt Mehitabel." With no pretense to sophistication, Aunt Mehitabel passed on to readers what she thought of the "nude statues" in the Capitol rotunda and the lack of beauty in the First Lady. Most Americans

In the White House Red Room, Nancy Reagan stands near the portrait of Angelica Van Buren, who acted as First Lady for her widowed father-in-law.

In this typical portrait of Julia Grant, she did not face the camera directly.

had seen Julia Grant only in photographs, and she almost always posed in profile to conceal the fact that her eyes were crossed.

Aunt Mehitabel, who attended one of Julia's afternoon receptions and realized that the curtains had been drawn so as to show the hostess in a dim light, set the record straight for her readers: "Mrs. Grant ain't a bit handsome. She ain't half as good lookin' as the pictures we see of her." Then, adding a touch of understanding, Aunt Mehitabel concluded: "I reckon it's another weakness of human nature to be watching her more than any other woman just because she's the lady of the White House."

Julia Grant's tenure coincided with an ebullient mood in the nation—a time that Mark Twain dubbed the "gilded age"—and no price tag seemed excessive. Twenty-nine-course dinners, extravagant flower arrangements, and expensive clothing fit right in with the times. Even Aunt Mehitabel, who reckoned the heights of buildings in haystacks, was enamored of the shiny gold wallpaper in her room at Washington's fashionable Willard Hotel.

National moods shift quickly, as Julia Grant's successor Lucy Hayes showed. Although the Hayes family had substantial personal wealth by the time Rutherford became president in 1877, Lucy emphasized humility and economy in her entertaining and in her public appearances. Americans responded by making her one of the most popular of all First Ladies, and historians ranked her in the top third.

The nation would repeatedly swing back and forth in its taste for "finer things" as opposed to "what common folks like," but in 1981, the swing was especially pronounced. Newly arrived First Lady Nancy Reagan made no apologies for liking elegance. Caviar and evening dresses with four-digit price tags showed up again in the State Dining Room after a lean period when Rosalynn Carter had served only wine, rather than hard liquor, and had played down the importance of expensive jewelry and a large wardrobe. When critics attacked her "queenly"

airs, Nancy responded in jest, saying she would never wear a crown because it mussed up her hair.

Lucy Hayes relaxed with her husband (standing), a family friend, and her dog at her Fremont, Ohio, home.

## Fine Furnishings for the Nation's House

The First Lady's individual style also shows up in the furnishings she chooses for the White House—to be distinguished from simple house-keeping supervision for which she is also responsible. Mamie Eisen-hower, who earned high accolades for her management of household staff, showed less interest in historic furnishings, and when Jacqueline Kennedy took her inspection tour in December 1960, she was disap-pointed by the mansion's appearance. Remembering her awe when she

When Abigail Adams moved into the White House in November 1800, it remained unfinished, but she made use of the large East Room to dry laundry.

had visited as a child of eleven, she resolved to restore some of the building's early elegance.

Actually, that elegance had developed rather slowly, and the first tenants complained loudly. Abigail and John Adams moved into the White House in November 1800, shortly before learning that they would be denied a second term. The results of the election remained in doubt for nearly three months, and not until the following February did Thomas Jefferson's victory become clear. Abigail accepted the outcome philosophically, writing her sister, "If we did not rise with ease, we can at least fall with grace, which," this astute woman noted, "is the more difficult task." Then, not waiting to see Jefferson inaugurated, she and her husband left the capital and returned to Massachusetts.

Abigail Adams's complaints about the President's House suggest she was not entirely sorry to leave it, although she had enough political savvy to confide only in trusted family and close friends. In a letter to her daughter, she lamented the wet plaster, the "mirrors fit for dwarfs," and the "barnlike" feeling of the whole structure. But she reminded daughter Abigail, "When asked how I like it, say that I wrote you the situation is beautiful."

With her usual resolution, Dolley Madison set to work in 1809 to furnish the bare rooms. Only Thomas Jefferson had resided there for a full term before the Madisons moved in, and he had not taken the time to furnish it as carefully as his beloved Monticello. Relying on the assistance of architect Benjamin Latrobe, whom Jefferson had appointed surveyor of public buildings, Dolley converted the large room on the west side, which Jefferson had used partially as an office and workroom, into the State Dining Room. Then she splurged most of the money that Congress had allotted her on it and the two adjoining rooms along the southern side—later known as the oval Blue Room and the Red Room. Latrobe persuaded her to forgo purchases in Europe in favor of Baltimore-made furniture in a style then known as "Grecian." For color, he suggested a sunny yellow for the parlor and rich red velvet for the draperies of the oval room.

Within months, the suite of rooms had been completed, and Dolley started a round of parties to show them off. Unfortunately, she had only a few years to enjoy the compliments. The nation was again at war with Britain, and in August 1814, before many visitors had a chance to admire her handiwork, British troops burned the President's House, but in doing so they provided her the opportunity to cement into public consciousness a First Lady's responsibility for looking after it.

Dolley had been warned that an attack on the capital was likely that late summer day, but she refused to budge until her husband, who had gone out inspecting troops, returned. Defiantly, she planned a dinner for forty and instructed the staff to lay the table and start cooking, as though she could stave off danger by refusing to acknowledge its presence.

Finally, around three in the afternoon, she was persuaded to leave, convinced by the argument that the nation would suffer more embarrassment if the president's wife were taken hostage than if news got out that she had fled in fear. Before she climbed into the carriage, however, she made one last walk through the rooms she had so carefully decorated, and she picked out a few of the items she thought most important to save.

Among the treasures was Gilbert Stuart's portrait of George Washington that would later hang in the East Room. The painting had been Congress's very first purchase for the President's House, and she thought it irreplaceable. Because it was so large, she ordered the canvas removed from its frame and rolled into a transportable scroll.

By the time the mansion was rebuilt and ready to be furnished again in 1817, James Monroe was president, and he and his wife, Elizabeth, set about the purchasing. They were not easily steered to American products. While living in Paris during James's stint as minister to France, they had developed a strong preference for French style and workmanship.

This portrait of Martha Washington, made in 1776, was her husband's favorite.

When Hillary Clinton refurbished the Blue Room she continued the tradition of featuring portraits of James (off-camera) and Elizabeth Monroe (center), emphasizing their important role in furnishing the White House in 1817. Also shown here is a portrait of James Madison (right).

They preferred French wine and literature, even spoke French with their daughters. The agent they engaged in Paris would buy for them—within limits. Congress had appropriated only twenty thousand dollars, and the Monroes had their own preferences. They requested lots of red and, with a nod to public approval, no "unclothed figures."

The Monroes set standards of elegance and fine craftsmanship that many of their successors would envy and emulate, but not without criticism. When their tastes outran their purse, they went back to Congress for more money. Until the new furniture arrived, they lent their own things, compensating themselves from the public treasury, but when word of that got out, they gave the money back. The whole affair became so complicated that it took a congressional commission to untangle it, and in the end it caused the president and First Lady considerable embarrassment. John Quincy Adams, who followed them into the White House, regretted that his predecessor had put himself in such a situation. Adams found it "almost as incongruous to the station of a president of the United States as it would be to a blooming virgin to exhibit herself naked before a multitude."

The scanty White House records that have survived show that the Monroes' careful selections eventually fell from public favor. By 1860, the dark glossy woods, pale marble, smooth silks, and polished brass trimmings associated with Empire and Directoire styles no longer fit in with most Americans' views of how they wanted their president to live. Tassels and velvet, dark colors, and potted ferns pleased them more. New woodworking machinery could now turn out intricate rococo designs, and imported rosewoods and mahoganies supplied the raw material for showing what the machines could do. One president's family after another refurnished the executive mansion until it was completely transformed from the light elegance and cheerful colors that early occupants preferred to heavy overstuffed Victorian opulence. Alice Roosevelt Longworth, the irreverent daughter of Theodore, later summed up its late-nineteenth-century decor as "steamboat parlor."

Kentucky-born Mary Lincoln spent money on the White House as though she thought she could disarm her critics by a demonstration of fine taste, but she succeeded only in making them hate her more. Even her normally patient husband became exasperated. After she had agreed to pay an enormous sum for new draperies and other nonessentials, he fumed, "It would stink in the nostrils of the American people" to have a president spend on "flub dubs for this damned old house" when the Union soldiers went without blankets.

Mary Lincoln's extravagant purchases for the White House resulted in some of its most treasured furnishings, including those in the Lincoln Bedroom, shown here with Nancy Reagan.

The large bed Mary purchased, however, remains one of the most treasured items in the White House. Eight feet long and six feet across, it was bought for the state guest bedroom and there is no evidence that either of the Lincolns ever slept in it. Its ornate carving, so common to the rococo styles of the mid-nineteenth century, fit in with the fringes and brocades so prized at the time.

In 1902, when structural reinforcements were required for safety, a First Lady with decidedly different tastes had a chance to alter the entire appearance of the executive mansion. Working with architect Charles McKim, Edith Roosevelt helped convert a Victorian White House into a colonial revival one. Although critics charged that the final result bore little resemblance to the interior a century earlier, it was more in line with the stately ceremonial style that Edith preferred. She successfully vetoed a plan to put red draperies in the large East Room, opting for the lighter yellow instead, and she approved a State Dining Room with oak paneling resembling an English manor house.

Her successors imposed their own tastes, making minor changes, and then Grace Coolidge set out to make permanent alterations. When Florence Harding moved her own things out following Warren's unexpected death in August 1923, the rooms of the private quarters were relatively empty and uninviting. Other presidential families had brought in favorite pieces from their homes or perhaps added a touch of Far Eastern exotic, but the Coolidges had always lived in rented quarters or furnished hotel apartments, and Grace had few resources on which to draw.

By the time Calvin won a full term of his own in 1924, Grace had formed plans to refurnish the state rooms in "American colonial" style and to do it carefully enough that she could proudly pass it on to her successors. She appointed an advisory committee, its members chosen from among the connoisseurs who had just completed a permanent exhibit of American furniture at New York's Metropolitan Museum. To finance the project, she turned to Congress for an increased appropria-

**Edith Roosevelt took a professional approach to managing the First Lady role.**

Grace Coolidge posed in one of her glamorous evening gowns.

tion of $50,000 (rather than the usual $20,000) and for a joint resolution permitting her to accept furniture and art donated to the White House. Like a museum curator, she asked wealthy Americans to help.

Very quickly, Grace Coolidge's project got out of hand. Members of her committee quarreled, and other architects and decorators got involved. When the controversy hit the newspapers, the president, whose frugal tendencies had made him skeptical of the project from the beginning, put a stop to further debate. He simply decreed that nothing would be done.

Lou Hoover, who followed Grace into the White House in 1929, came with far more personal resources. After managing several large homes around the world, she had her own strong preferences and sometimes joked that she had never seen a room she did not want to change. With her take-charge personality, she frequently annoyed the staff with her many requests (one employee wondered if she would be moving the staircases next), but she insisted that the White House be a peaceful, attractive setting for her husband to do his best work.

An extremely intelligent woman, Lou had lived in China, where she became a shrewd collector of antique porcelains, but she also had an eye for fine American things. In Fredericksburg, Virginia, she had visited the James Monroe Law Office Museum and admired the exquisite furniture that Monroe descendants had put on display there. Since she could not hope to acquire those pieces, she resolved to have them copied by master craftsmen for her parlor on the second floor of the White House.

Lou's assistant reported that her boss took "delighted interest" in filling the room "with true pieces of the period": she raided the mansion's storerooms in search of furniture dating from the time the Monroes had lived there. Lou thought that, as the first full-term residents of the White House after it was rebuilt, Elizabeth and James Monroe ought to be identified with it in a special way, so the "Monroe suite," on the second floor, became the first to be restored to early-nineteenth-century elegance.

Eleanor Roosevelt (1933–1945), who lived there the longest of any First Lady, showed little interest in interior decorating. Furnishing for comfort rather than elegance had always been her rule, and at her Val Kill cottage at Hyde Park, overstuffed furniture in noncoordinated patterns served her well enough. She much preferred to concentrate her attention on the conversation of the people who sat on those chairs, and she gave her time and energy to causes rather than fabric samples. Besides, her tenure coincided with the Great Depression and World War II, inauspicious times to talk about decorating.

Although necessary major structural changes were made during the Truman years, the decor of the White House did not change significantly until the 1960s, when Jacqueline Kennedy embarked on her well-publicized restoration (she did not like the term "redecoration"). The young president's wife showed enormous enthusiasm for the project and went herself, in working clothes, to the storerooms where old pieces were kept. Rummaging around, she located furniture and artwork that had not been viewed for years. An elaborate gilded centerpiece, purchased by the Monroes but typically reserved for the most important guests, went on permanent exhibit in the State Dining Room. Many of the vermeil pieces were displayed throughout the state rooms.

Turning to others for help, Jacqueline Kennedy borrowed Lorraine Pearce, a curator from the Smithsonian Institution, to catalog all the holdings, and she formed the White House Historical Association for the express purpose of increasing "understanding, appreciation, and enjoyment" of the President's House. To help raise money for her restoration, she arranged for guidebooks to be sold on the premises. Although some critics complained that selling anything within the presidential residence commercialized it and cheapened it, she stood her ground, and more than one million books were sold in the first two years.

Not all observers approved Jacqueline Kennedy's choices. Some people thought her approach too Frenchified, and they objected that she

Eleanor Roosevelt welcomed Madame Chiang Kai-shek to the White House in 1943.

should not have relied so heavily on the advice of Stephane Boudin, whose experience had been limited to Napoleon's imperial château at Malmaison and other grand French houses. But the popular First Lady acted as a magnet to visitors, and the tourist lines at the east entrance grew long.

The televised tour that Jacqueline Kennedy conducted in early 1962 called so much glowing attention to the White House that Lady Bird Johnson pronounced it a daunting act to follow. The First Lady from Texas solicited artworks and antiques to round out the collection, but she hesitated to make major changes—even to remove the plaque that her predecessor had placed above a mantel, citing the "one thousand days that President John Kennedy and his wife, Jacqueline," lived there.

A determined Pat Nixon (1969–1974) turned to Clement Conger, who had made a name for himself by directing the refurbishing of the diplomatic reception rooms at the State Department. Working together over a period of five years, the energetic First Lady and the knowledge-able curator quietly managed to acquire more antiques for the White House than had been gathered during the Kennedy and Johnson admin-istrations combined. A 1961 law, which forbade selling or disposing of White House holdings, encouraged many Americans to donate precious furniture and art now that it would not be given away at the president's whim.

Although Rosalynn Carter (1977–1981) worked closely with the Committee for the Preservation of the White House and helped add many American paintings to the White House collection, she did not leave her personal imprint on the executive mansion. Like Eleanor Roosevelt, she preferred to concentrate her energies elsewhere, and that attitude may have motivated her successor to focus on the residence. Newspapers reported that Nancy Reagan (1981–1989) could hardly wait to start her decorators working, and she hinted that the Carters might cooperate by vacating before Ronald Reagan was sworn in. When

Jacqueline Kennedy's White House restoration had its unglamorous side—here she helps a workman install a candelabra. *(above)* **Lady Bird Johnson, assisted by Chief Usher J. B. West, explained White House details to her successor Pat Nixon.** *(opposite)*

Grace Coolidge became famous for clowning in front of cameras. *(above)* **Decades before becoming First Lady, Florence Harding posed with her dog, Jumbo, in front of her Marion, Ohio, home.** *(opposite)*

they demurred, remaining until the traditional January 20 move-out date, she continued with her planning, hiring society decorator Ted Graber to direct the project.

The nearly one million-dollar price tag on the final product raised some eyebrows, although Nancy Reagan quickly pointed out that the funds had come from private donations and that the china had been so depleted that she had to mix and match sets for large dinners. Her critics were not mollified. They argued that the donors had gained tax advantages of giving to the White House and probably hoped for friendly treatment from the president.

Nancy's successors were more grateful, and they thanked her publicly for making their own tenures easier. The new wall coverings, updated bathrooms, and refinished doors and floors that she passed on to them meant that Barbara Bush and Hillary Rodham Clinton faced only minor refurbishing. But the American public never quite forgave Nancy for what they considered to be excessive spending, and her husband's announcement that she had taken a "bum rap" did little to placate them.

## White House Pets

In redecorating the White House, First Ladies have to make room for the family pet, because most administrations bring a favorite with them. By the time they leave, it is almost as well-known as the family itself. Presidents' pets are among the most photographed animals on earth (unless they are declared "off limits," like Socks, the Clintons' cat) and Americans retain a fondness for them long after their masters leave office. Franklin Roosevelt's Scotty, Fala, inspired comment half a century after the president had died.

Several White House animals have been closely associated with First Ladies. Betty Ford released photographs of her golden retriever, "Liberty," with her new pups; Nancy Reagan often walked across the South Lawn with her King Charles spaniel pulling at his leash; and Barbara Bush

Barbara Bush's dog, Millie (on chair), contemplates the portrait of a predecessor, Grace Coolidge's Rob Roy.

turned her spaniel, Millie, into the most famous dog in America.

In an earlier era, only Washingtonians or visitors to the capital knew about Dolley Madison's pet macaw, but an entire nation delighted in Grace Coolidge's menagerie. The most popular First Lady of the 1920s was photographed with her pet raccoon, Rebecca, and her dog, Rob Roy, named as a joke on the Prohibition decade when Rob Roy cocktails were illegal. When time came for her official portrait, Grace posed with her dog beside her.

## Reflecting National Themes

Although every president's wife wants her family to live as comfortably as possible in the White House, each is reminded that this is the nation's house provided for short-term tenants. Beyond the family's own personal tastes, the house ought to reflect an entire nation and its shifting preferences.

The Hayes administration coincided with an increased attention to national themes, and Lucy honored the shift by her choice of White House china. While other First Ladies had selected more elegant and regal patterns, with golden borders and crested bands, she approved the purchase of china depicting plants and animals. The young artist who had drawn the designs wanted to include all flora and fauna known to the continent, and he appears to have missed very few. The Hayes china is unique—a celebration of America's natural beauty rather than its acquired power or wealth.

The celebration is not entirely accidental. The Hayes presidency resulted from a compromise worked out to end the occupation of former Confederate states after the Civil War ended. In a committee decision about how to count disputed votes in the electoral college, a strategy was devised to make Rutherford Hayes the winner in return for his promise to withdraw Union troops from the South. It was a somber time, the nation's deep war wounds still in need of healing, and Lucy

Hayes's emphasis on what the United States shared rather than the power of the victorious Union was both telling and wise.

Caroline Harrison entered the White House in 1889 just as themes of national greatness and world recognition reached new heights. The 1890s celebrated what the United States had done, as the nation embarked on international adventures amid debates on the "closing of the frontier." It was a time for Americans, feeling good about themselves, to emphasize their uniqueness—a nation of sixty-three million whose ancestors had taken control of the continent in an incredibly short time. Very few people questioned the rightness of that domination, and most gloated over the speed with which it had been accomplished.

An avid painter, Caroline Harrison designed a White House china pattern incorporating a corn-and-goldenrod border, and she worked the acorn design into her inaugural gown. The entire Harrison family made a point of announcing that their clothing had been made in the U.S.A.

Twentieth-century First Ladies returned to regal themes, and borders of gold predominated in their choice of china. Even the egalitarian-minded Eleanor Roosevelt selected a porcelain service that combined the seal of the President of the United States with the Roosevelt family crest (all in gold). Bess Truman, for all her emphasis on personal humility, thought it appropriate that the president's table be set with plates featuring a wide gold banner.

Jacqueline Kennedy purchased no new china service, and then Lady Bird Johnson selected a pattern featuring delicate wildflowers. In 1962 Rachel Carson's book, *Silent Spring,* warning that maltreatment of the environment could mute birds in springtime, had just been published, and many Americans were beginning to voice their worries about the environment. Nancy Reagan later pronounced the Johnson china too informal for state dinners, but it reflected Lady Bird's strong personal interest as well as national interest in the environment.

White House observers watched carefully to see what alterations

Had Caroline Harrison gotten her way, the White House would have been enlarged and altered in the 1890s.

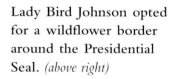

Edith Wilson's idea for setting aside a room to display presidential china appealed to her successors. *(opposite left)*

China selected by James and Elizabeth Monroe was made in France and featured the American eagle. *(above left)*

Nancy Reagan's choice, featuring the Presidential Seal at center and a wide red rim, was American-made, by Lenox. *(above center)*

Lady Bird Johnson opted for a wildflower border around the Presidential Seal. *(above right)*

The turkey platter *(center)* is part of a service Lucy Hayes ordered for the White House in 1879.

As the young bride of President John Tyler, Julia Tyler often emphasized regal settings.

Hillary Rodham Clinton would approve. Her press secretary reported that the First Lady had prepared by reading several dozen volumes on the mansion's history, and by November 1993, the changes were ready for inspection—or at least most of them were. Her daughter Chelsea's room was declared "off limits" to reporters. With about $400,000 in private funds, Hillary's decorator from Little Rock had returned the Lincoln Sitting Room and the Treaty Room to the Victorian opulence of an earlier time, using what the press described as "blood-red fabrics," multiple patterns, and heavy walnut furniture, including additional bookcases that the Clintons required. In describing what she had done, Hillary's decorator characterized her clients' taste as full of "personal energy" and "very today." She played down the cost, noting that she had recycled wallpaper and draperies from an exhibition in Little Rock.

## Regal Styles

Hillary Clinton's emphasis on comfort and economy, along with her reputation for professional competence, contrasted with some of her "queenly" predecessors. More than a century earlier, a parade of presidents' wives (and other female relatives) developed a series of regal settings in which to present themselves. Julia Gardiner Tyler (1844–1845) drove around the capital with "finer horses than those of the Russian minister" and received guests seated in "a large armchair on a slightly raised platform." To add a royal touch to her husband's appearances, she instructed the band to play "Hail to the Chief," a piece that became closely associated with the president. Her own attire came about as close to a queen's as is possible in a democracy—she wore three feathers in her hair and a long dress with a train in royal purple.

Julia had no doubt been inspired by the example of one of her immediate predecessors—Angelica Van Buren, who served as White House hostess for her widowed father-in-law, Martin Van Buren (1837–1841). Angelica married the oldest of the four Van Buren sons a few months after being introduced to him by her cousin Dolley Madison. On a grand wedding tour of the continent, the newlyweds, as the son and daughter-in-law of the American president, were treated like royalty, and Angelica took note of how European monarchs distanced themselves from commoners. Queens never shook hands, and they often seated themselves on a platform, surrounded by a tableau formation of ladies-in-waiting while adoring subjects filed by in respectful silence. When Angelica returned to Washington, she staged a similar production in the oval room of the White House and won wide public approval. Surrounding herself with a bevy of young women friends in flowing white dresses, she invited visitors to walk by and view them.

Mary Lincoln refrained from presenting tableaux, but she liked tiaras fashioned out of flowers and never shied away from entertaining royalty. When other Washington women, more sophisticated and well traveled than she, offered to manage a dinner for the visiting son of Emperor Napoleon III of France, Mary insisted she could handle it herself. Although born and raised in Kentucky, she had attended an academy where French was spoken, and her grandmother read Voltaire in the original. As Mary later told it, she made a hit with Prince Napoleon, and after the party he turned to her in some surprise and said, "Paris is not all the world."

Royal visits proliferated in the twentieth century and the White House staff came to take them in stride, paying little more attention to a titled guest than to a celebrity from the entertainment or sports world. But the visit of King George VI and Queen Elizabeth of England in June 1939 was something special. No reigning British monarch had ever visited the United States, and excitement ran high. Cleaning staff went on double time to scrub the executive mansion into top shape, and reporters queried the First Lady about what she would wear and whether or not she would curtsey.

When word got out that Eleanor Roosevelt had invited the royal

In this, the first photograph ever made of an incumbent First Lady, Julia Tyler looked remarkably ordinary.

couple to Hyde Park, where she intended to feed them hot dogs at a cookout, her mother-in-law forwarded a letter of protest that someone had sent her, noting on the back, "Only one of many such that I have received." But all attempts to persuade Eleanor to serve more regal fare failed, and plans went ahead for an informal picnic at Hyde Park. The king and queen were delighted, and the First Lady later pronounced their visit a great success.

## Paying the Bills

With no royal purse to pay the bills, presidents' wives must worry about what things cost. Starting in 1789 at $25,000, the chief executive's salary doubled in 1873 and then rose to $75,000 in 1909. By 1949 it was set at $100,000, which was doubled in 1969. Although that might seem adequate to most Americans, especially when the president's entertaining is paid for by Congress, with monies earmarked for that purpose, or by the State Department and political party committees, First Ladies have objected repeatedly to having to stretch to meet their official obligations.

Abigail Adams lamented the cost of entertaining (and the price of rum) nearly two centuries before Nancy Reagan lodged a similar complaint. Nobody had told her, Nancy wrote, "that the president and his wife are charged for every meal, as well as for such incidentals as dry cleaning, tooth paste and other toiletries." She suspected most Americans believed, as she had, that the government paid for everything consumed in the White House, but as she learned, that is not true.

Few chief executives have had large personal fortunes, and more than one left office poorer than when he came in. It frequently fell to his wife to see that he did not. Abigail Adams was particularly successful in this regard, and her grandson, the diplomat Charles Francis Adams, wrote that she had helped keep the family solvent by running their Massachusetts farm so well. As "a farmer cultivating the land and dis-

Roosevelt family money (both Eleanor's and her husband's) relieved her of financial worries during her twelve-year tenure as First Lady.

Edith Roosevelt (shown here with her youngest son, Quentin) made shrewd managerial decisions as First Lady, then concentrated on time with her family.

cussing the weather and the crops; a merchant reporting prices current and rates of exchange and directing the making up of invoices," she had made enough money so that the Adams men could pursue politics.

James Monroe was not so fortunate. His wife, Elizabeth, spent large sums for her own wardrobe, often ordered from Paris. According to one report, she paid $1,500 for a single outfit, when most Americans did not earn that amount in a lifetime, and she showed little ability to cut corners in running her household. No wonder James Monroe died a poor man.

After 1829, when it became more common for men of modest means to reach the presidency, their wives often struggled to pay the bills. Each faced a balancing act: entertaining in style without dipping too deeply into their own purses. Edith Roosevelt, although one of the wealthier, realized she might be embarrassed if the president were outshone. Yet she knew the folly of trying to outbid other Washington wives with large personal fortunes, and she decided to take a stand on cost control. The strategy she devised, discontinued when she left office, involved holding weekly meetings with the wives of cabinet members. More than sewing circles or tea parties, the discussions subtly set limits for entertaining so that wives who might have had the means or a hankering to outdo the White House in some social event would restrain themselves.

Edith Roosevelt surprised some of her aides by deciding that bits and pieces of presidential china would no longer be given away to friends or auctioned to the highest bidder—they would be broken and thrown into the Potomac, a more appropriate way of disposing of them, she thought. Archie Butt, an admiring aide who later died when the SS *Titanic* went down, helped carry out Edith's decrees, although it saddened him. "When I think how I should value even one piece of it, it hurts to smash it," he wrote his mother, "but I am sure it is the only right thing to do."

Edith, whose own family had lost its considerable fortune when she was young, tended to worry about money. But in the White House, she saved herself some trouble by engaging a caterer to serve official dinners at a cost of $7.50 per person. Although that figure seemed high—a sales clerk did not earn that amount in a week—the arrangement freed the First Lady from the obligation to hire and train a staff who might be needed only a few weeks out of the entire year.

Her successor, Helen Herron Taft, competed with the Roosevelts in many ways. As Alice Roosevelt Longworth put it, "Her ideas were rather grander than ours." Mrs. Taft hired a housekeeper, Elizabeth Jaffray, to oversee purchasing and staff, because, she explained, "I wanted a woman who could relieve me of the supervision of such details as no man, expert steward though he might be, would ever recognize."

One of Jaffray's goals was economy because Helen Taft insisted on saving money. When she learned that the president's salary would be increased by $25,000, she vowed to save the entire sum for her family. In this, as in most things that she attempted, she succeeded, and her husband boasted that she had banked $80,000 the first two years, which he termed "a pretty good sum."

Part of Helen Taft's savings resulted from gifts. For an extravagant celebration of the Tafts' silver wedding anniversary in 1911, she did not discourage presents, and since she sent out several thousand invitations, she assured herself substantial returns. Businessmen eager to make a good impression on the president vied with each other to be generous. One White House employee confessed that he had not known so much silver existed in the world. The head of U.S. Steel, who had only a casual acquaintance with the Tafts, sent a tureen valued at $8,000, and other guests murmured among themselves about what each had "put up." In her practical way, Helen Taft recycled some valuable pieces, erasing the monograms and passing them on rather than digging into her own pocket to buy gifts for others.

Mamie Eisenhower earned high praise for her careful White House management.

## Working with Staff

Helen Taft also made staff changes, dismissing employees who had long served the presidential household. Although her predecessor Edith Roosevelt thought she treated loyal employees shabbily, Helen was simply following tradition that the president's wife takes charge of the domestic staff. The first occupants brought their own personal servants —or, in the case of a few southerners (including the Madisons, Polks, and Taylors), their slaves—to look after the cooking and cleaning at the presidential mansion. Gradually the pattern changed as the nation grew and the functions of the White House expanded. Although a few trusted employees still accompanied the chief executive's family, the bulk of the work was handled by permanent employees who stayed on from one administration to the next and saw themselves serving the nation rather than temporary residents.

Of course, the staff had their favorites, and the First Lady's management style became the source of comment in each administration. Mamie Eisenhower was remembered as a demanding boss but a kind one. She had long experience as a military wife and had managed households from the Philippines to New York City. Known to inspect windowsills military style by passing a white-gloved hand across them as she passed through a room, she caused some grumbling from employees accustomed to the more relaxed housekeeping styles of Eleanor Roosevelt and Bess Truman. J. B. West, who was assistant chief usher at the time, drew a connection between Mamie's management and her military background. She had a "spine of steel," West wrote, and "could give orders staccato crisp, detailed and final, as if it were she who had been a five-star general."

Lou Hoover, like Mamie, was Iowa born, but put her imprint on the job in a different way. In managing homes around the world, she had developed some unique techniques for efficiency, and she tried to implement them in the White House. Having lived in China, the Hoovers sometimes used Mandarin to communicate privately, and Lou relied on a complicated system of hand movements to signal her servants. One raised finger might mean to refill the glasses; another gesture conveyed a need to move the guests along more quickly. Bewildered servants found the communications unclear; they would miss them or interpret them incorrectly, thus incurring the wrath of a First Lady who made high demands on herself and others as well.

The kitchen crew in the Hoover White House worked particularly hard. Lou and Bert (as she always called him) dressed for dinner every evening and ate in the State Dining Room, so even if there had been no guests, the staff would have been pressed to perform more carefully than if only a tray upstairs had been requested. But in fact, the Hoovers pre-

Grace Coolidge, who did most of her own housework before moving to Washington, was often teased by her husband, who suggested she share her piecrust recipe with street pavers.

ferred company at mealtime, and one employee insisted that they dined alone only once a year, on their wedding anniversary.

At any other time, a guest list could grow very long on extremely short notice. Ava Long, the head housekeeper, complained in print that she often prepared for half a dozen expected dinner guests and then had to make do for three times that number. On one occasion, after she had improvised a concoction of leftovers to serve an unexpected crowd, one guest requested the recipe, and Long supplied it, along with the name she had sarcastically attached: "White House Surprise Supreme."

Although Lou Hoover's reputation for personal kindness was legend, her efficient management style did not appeal to many White House employees who preferred the casual, sunny approach of her immediate predecessor, Grace Coolidge. The Coolidges had always lived very modestly, and Grace had never directed a sizable domestic staff before. She resorted to a kind of "we're in this together" style that encouraged chumminess and gave the staff a sense of equality with the president's family—an elevation that many found to their liking.

Eleanor Roosevelt had always lived in homes with many servants, but after her marriage she relied on her mother-in-law to manage many of the household details. Henrietta Nesbitt, the Hudson Valley housewife whom Eleanor engaged to oversee food preparation at the White House, quickly achieved a reputation as one of the most irascible and least liked of all those who ever held the job. Eleanor's adult children recalled Nesbitt's meals with little pleasure, and the convivial president (who had to face her meals more often than they) was driven to exasperation. Nesbitt's menus were as lacking in color and imagination as they were in taste, and when politely requested to change, she stonewalled and continued to do as she pleased. Franklin Roosevelt's request for less broccoli (after being served it on successive days) brought more of the same. Nesbitt explained to her staff that broccoli "was good for him" and he should "learn to like it." In the next administration, the normally

patient Bess Truman fired Nesbitt.

Broccoli has figured more than once in discussions of presidents' preferences. George Bush announced jokingly that he had eaten it all his life, but as president, he intended to stop because he had never liked it. The Bushes' chef was considerably more agreeable than Nesbitt, and the vegetable disappeared from White House menus until the Clintons moved in and put it on their list of favorites. ("Broccoli's in," the *New York Times* reported early in 1993.)

Cooking for the president remains a sure route to fame and fortune. Cookbooks, television appearances, and offers from top-paying restaurants often reward a stint in the president's basement kitchen. But while the First Lady may be making a cook's career, she also has to suit her own tastes and please her family.

Jacqueline Kennedy, following her preference for things French, engaged René Verdon, who had been trained in his native France and

Although she took little personal interest in food, Pat Nixon conferred with White House chefs on plans for important dinners.

"Broccoli's in" at the Clinton White House, announced the caption for this front-page picture of Hillary Rodham Clinton.

worked three years in New York city restaurants. He was apparently not her first choice: rumors circulated that the First Lady had tried unsuccessfully to lure a Vietnamese chef away from the French ambassador's residence in London. Verdon's debut in April 1961 merited a photograph on the front page of the *New York Times* along with a story about the very French menu he had served the Kennedys' eighteen luncheon guests: trout with sauce Vincent, beef *au jus,* artichoke bottoms Beaucaire, asparagus with sauce Maltaise, and *vacherine desir d'avril.*

Verdon stayed on after the Johnsons moved into the White House in late 1963, but with them, he fared less well. Instead of turning out the quenelles and lobster mousse that the Kennedys preferred, he was called on to cook Texas style with garbanzos and chili peppers, items not previously in his repertoire. Guests complained of deteriorating standards and rather unorthodox combinations, such as red snapper and cold beets. By December 1965, Verdon announced he would be moving on, to open his own restaurant in San Francisco.

Lady Bird Johnson relied on Zephyr Wright to cook for the family. She had been making the Johnsons' favorites for years and knew all their preferences: yellow lemon birthday cakes and strawberry meringues, turkey dressing and steaks, fried chicken and chili. Wright was also charged with rationing the president's calories when doctors insisted he shed a few pounds, and when she had to be absent because of illness or a family emergency, Lady Bird described it as a "sizable crisis. She's hard to get along without."

Besides the domestic staff (which by the 1990s had grown to nearly one hundred, including cleaners, carpenters, butlers, and florists), the curatorial staff also comes under the First Lady's aegis. A chief curator, appointed by the president, and a staff of several assistants work in cramped basement quarters to help coordinate the cataloging and exhibition of artworks and furniture in the White House collection. It is this staff that helps each new First Lady (and her interior designer if she uses one) select the furniture and pictures that she wants around her family on the second floor and the pieces she would rather keep at a distance.

The entire White House operation, including the skilled and professional staffs, is known for its competence, and First Ladies have been particularly effusive in complimenting employees on their expertise. When Betty Ford moved in on short notice in 1974, she faced a grueling schedule, including a state dinner ten days away. But the staff took care of everything, leading Mrs. Ford to say, "All you have to do is decide what you want and say it—there are plenty of people to see that it gets done." Nancy Reagan had few regrets about retiring to California in 1989, except for leaving behind the unique luxury provided by the White House staff.

## Responsibility for the Mansion

While the staff remain anonymous, unrecognized by the American public, the First Lady's face is known to all, and she takes ultimate responsibility for how things run and how they look. Martha Washington apparently played no part in the design of the original White House; a commission selected the winning architect from among seven competitors. The first changes to the structure were the result of presidential, not First Lady decisions: under Thomas Jefferson, wings were added to both sides; then James Monroe oversaw the addition of the south portico, and Andrew Jackson took credit for the north portico.

But when it comes to allocation of space and modernization, the distaff side of the White House is often heard. In 1848 Sarah Polk went along with Congress's decision to install gas lights but, worried that they would not function adequately, she retained an old chandelier. When the gas lights suddenly went out at an important reception, she called for the candles to be lit. More than forty years later, Caroline Harrison, who failed in her plan to significantly enlarge the mansion, did manage to have electric lights installed. Servants reported, however, that the

Rosalynn Carter, shown here with the New York Metropolitan Singers/Greek Choral Society, found ways for more Americans to participate in White House entertainment.

Harrisons were so uncomfortable with electricity that they refused to touch the switches themselves and called employees to turn the lights on and off.

Presidents' wives were involved in each of the major renovations of the twentieth century. In 1902, Edith Roosevelt agreed to the addition of the new West Wing, and in 1927, Grace Coolidge cooperated with an expansion that pushed up the roof behind a balustrade in order to accommodate an additional floor. In 1949, Bess Truman made a rare public announcement to endorse the idea of remodeling the old building rather than scrapping it to construct a new marble palace (as some had suggested). She was persuaded of the need for action when one of the engineers warned her that the second floor was staying in place mostly "from force of habit."

## Arranging Entertainment

Structural damage is bound to occur when thousands of guests move in and out of the building every year, but a president's popularity is sometimes related to the number of people he greets and entertains. A shrewd First Lady is a busy hostess. Abigail Adams set an early precedent when she arranged for the Marine Band to play in the second-floor oval room on New Year's Day 1801, only a month after she had moved in.

Later presidents resorted to outdoor concerts so as to accommodate more people, and then Rutherford and Lucy Hayes began the custom of scheduling musicales for invited guests. Edith Roosevelt varied the programs and included both world-famous artists such as the great pianist Paderewski and lesser-known local performers. When an amateur German chorus sang, Edith listened smilingly, only later confiding to her daughter that the smell of garlic and beer that came from the direction of the performers had almost overwhelmed her.

Edith received so many requests to perform at the White House that she sought professional advice on whom she should schedule. Other

First Ladies would do the same. None wanted to offend an important congressman or contributor by denying them or their friends a chance to perform. For many years a representative from piano manufacturers Steinway & Sons auditioned unknown musicians and offered advice, letting the First Lady off the hook. She remained, however, the ultimate arbiter.

An invitation to perform at the White House could boost a career. Eleanor Roosevelt opened opportunities for a woman conductor, Antonia Brico, to perform in major halls, and Jacqueline Kennedy provided opera singer Grace Bumbry with a special occasion on which to make her American debut. Other First Ladies bestowed a stamp of approval on their own personal favorites (Mamie Eisenhower featured Lawrence Welk) or tried to reflect the variety in national tastes (Barbara Bush scheduled the Beach Boys).

## Using the White House as Backdrop for Good Causes

The White House also launches charitable drives. Its stately porticos and elegant oval rooms provide a superb backdrop for poster children and recognition ceremonies, and as chief keeper of the White House, the First Lady is often called on to pose, shake hands, or open a fund-raising drive. In the nation's early decades, the president's wife was usually identified with local causes, since people outside the capital rarely saw her or knew what she looked like. Dolley Madison, who took such avid interest in entertaining, also recognized a responsibility to help others, and she accepted the job of directress of the newly established Orphans' Asylum.

By the 1870s, the First Lady had gone national. Magazines had developed nationwide circulation, and many more women—whose literacy rates finally equaled men's—bought them. Editors reached out to the new market by hiring women writers who tailored their articles to

Grace Coolidge, in the uniform of a Red Cross nurse, met with wounded servicemen.

In 1880, Lucy Hayes (seated in carriage) accompanied the president to the West Coast and posed for this picture in Yosemite. *(above)* Although thousands of Americans visited the White House during the Nixon presidency, Pat Nixon understood that for many of them it was a first and only visit—and it had to be special. *(opposite)*

the interests of female readers. Presidents' wives gained more popularity than most of them wanted, and Caroline Harrison was besieged with requests for scraps of her old dresses (to be worked into quilts) and locks of her hair (for who knows what sentimental exhibition).

In 1880, Lucy Hayes became the first president's wife to travel across the continent, and as she did so she was greeted as a national heroine and entreated to champion "good causes" of all kinds. Caroline Harrison agreed to work for the establishment of the Johns Hopkins Medical School, and she served as first president of the Daughters of the American Revolution when it was started in 1890.

Bess Truman could make the shyest visitor feel important.

A few organizations, such as the American Red Cross and the Girl Scouts, became so closely associated with the First Lady that they seemed almost part of the job. The idea that the Red Cross had its own patron saint at 1600 Pennsylvania Avenue extends back to the early 1900s, when William Howard Taft served as the organization's president, and many First Ladies lent their names to it, chairing benefits and special drives. When Eleanor Roosevelt traveled to the South Pacific, she wore the Red Cross uniform.

Other organizations, smaller and less closely associated with the White House, also request endorsements. It is usually the First Lady, rather than the president, who obliges. The March of Dimes Birth Defects Foundation, actually started by Franklin Roosevelt as the National Foundation for Infantile Paralysis, typically enlists the president's wife to pose with the annual poster child. The American Heart Association, American Cancer Society, and a long list of other organizations prevail on the nation's most prominent woman for a photograph.

Bess Truman (1945–1953), who remained a private person throughout nearly eight years of very public life, merited only a few mentions in the press—when she made a trip to Independence, caught a cold, or assisted in some charitable cause. But for a reticent First Lady, she compiled a lengthy list of appearances, many of them at the White House. She greeted leaders of the Camp Fire Girls, launched cookie drives for the Girl Scouts, and entertained wounded service men.

Mamie Eisenhower (1953–1961) took second place to none in her charitable work. By the 1950s, the number of organizations had mushroomed, and her schedule looked like an encyclopedia of the new and the old. Besides those her predecessors had assisted, Mamie also made time for lending a hand to the Community Chest, the Lighthouse for the Blind, and many others.

Pat Nixon (1969–1974), famous for her promise to open the White House "to the little guys," made good on her word. She invited senior citizens for Thanksgiving dinner, and to accommodate disabled people, she set up special tours. A blind youngster was permitted to touch an important piece of sculpture or furniture that other, sighted individuals could not. People in wheel-chairs and on crutches were all welcomed.

## Nation's House

Like so many other customs, the use of the mansion as a national center extends all the way back to the first occupants. Dolley Madison received callers every Wednesday evening and widened the invitation so that any-one who had been presented to the president (or knew someone who had) felt free to attend. Sometimes crowds turned up, and Dolley's crit-ics thought she had gone too far. Andrew Jackson, whose wife had died just months before his inauguration, entered on his presidential duties with heavy heart, but not so heavy as to ignore the people who had sent him there. He opened it to the public for his inauguration party, which drew thousands, causing Washington establishment to grumble about the "crush" of democracy.

A century later, when many more Americans could travel to Washington (and most of them had the White House at the top of their lists of places to see), First Ladies became better known. James Hagerty, who served as Dwight Eisenhower's press secretary in the 1950s, recalled that as a child he had gone with his family to the capital and that his strongest memory had been of Grace Coolidge. But as the number of visitors increased, not even the most energetic First Lady could person-ally greet everyone who passed through. Long invitation lists were drawn up to accommodate as many people as possible.

Eleanor Roosevelt used her White House press conferences to com-municate with the nation, much as her husband used his "fireside chats." Within hours of Franklin's first inauguration, well before the new pres-ident greeted reporters, she invited women journalists to talk with her in the Monroe Room. Although she insisted that she would not touch

Eleanor Roosevelt presided over the Easter egg roll on the White House lawn, a tradition dating back to Lucy Hayes.

**Betty Ford relished a rare quiet moment in the White House.**

political subjects, she quickly broke that rule, and when she inadvertently revealed that the White House would resume serving alcoholic beverages in 1934, reporters knew that Prohibition had effectively ended. News services without a woman on staff rushed to hire one, so as not to miss any more scoops from the First Lady.

Eventually, reporters' easy access to the White House had to be limited—as did everyone's. By the 1970s, terrorists and publicity seekers proved such a threat that a concrete barrier was erected to bar vehicles that might carry explosives. Metal detectors "approved" each tourist, and staff members who had worked there for decades learned to wear identification cards around their necks. Rosalynn Carter, in attempting to compensate for the changes, arranged that concerts be televised so that the entire nation could be invited. Special telecasts of "An Evening at the White House" enabled millions of Americans to "attend" the same performance as the presidential family.

## First Ladies' Exhibition Gallery

To acknowledge the work that presidents' wives do, Edith Roosevelt decided to feature them in a portrait gallery. She ordered their pictures ("Myself included," she specified) displayed on the first floor of the White House. Even before proceeding to the main floor, each visitor entering, whether on one of the daily tours or in response to a personal invitation, would be reminded of the role of First Ladies. It has become customary for recent occupants to hold the most visible spots, in the ground-floor corridor leading to the main stairway. The most famous portraits, such as that of Jacqueline Kennedy by Aaron Shikler, are placed strategically to gain maximum attention.

Not far away from the White House, another First Ladies Hall draws attention to their records. The Smithsonian Institution's exhibit of gowns got a boost from Mamie Eisenhower, who initiated the custom of each president's wife adding her inaugural gown to the collection. Before

1953, donations had been on an ad hoc basis, and each woman made her own decision about which dress to give the Smithsonian and when to give it. Bess Truman had turned over her inaugural outfit just weeks before retiring to Missouri, but Mamie seemed eager to set a precedent, and in November 1953, before she had been in the job a full year, she turned over her pink silk gown, embroidered with more than two thousand rhinestones.

The First Ladies exhibit soon became the most popular in the Smithsonian's Museum of American History, and when it was redesigned in the early 1990s to emphasize actions rather than clothes, it continued to draw crowds. Viewers could now listen to Lou Hoover's and Eleanor Roosevelt's radio speeches and explore Lady Bird Johnson's environmental work. Betty Ford applauded the change, and when she first saw the new exhibit, she pronounced herself grateful: "Now I will be remembered for what I did," she said, "rather than what I wore."

...........................................................................

In fact, Betty Ford will be remembered for both, because Americans find it difficult to separate a First Lady's ceremonial presence from her concern for good works and her stands on important issues. With the palatial White House as backdrop, she demonstrates the curious contradictions of her job. A nation created out of a distrust of monarchy developed a substitute that looked very much like it—a temporary throne for the wife of whatever man is elected president for a four-year term.

A First Lady's ceremonial appearances serve as "rallying point for a nation's feelings," it has been observed. Much as she might like to escape the role, abdication is not encouraged. She can decide for herself how to exercise the power that the job brings, but she will be encouraged not to squander it. "Each First Lady is given a magic wand," one old Washington hand observed, "but nobody tells her how to use it. Each woman has to figure that out for herself."

Helen Taft had this coat embroidered in China *(opposite left)*. Taft coat embroidery detail *(opposite lower right)*. Florence Harding, one of the oldest women to serve as First Lady, often dressed like a Hollywood starlet *(opposite right)*. Caroline Harrison stressed American themes and workmanship in her inaugural gown *(above left)*. Frances Cleveland, one of the youngest First Ladies, was widely copied in fashion and style *(above right)*.

# *Leader of Women*

When Andrew Jackson ran for president in 1828, some Americans questioned his wife's fitness to "sit at the head of female society." More than a century later, another military wife, Mamie Eisenhower, faced charges that she drank too much. Their husbands defended them, but neither woman attempted to counter the accusations at the time. Each realized that, whether she liked it or not, wives are evaluated along with the candidates, as

The young and popular Frances Cleveland posed for this photograph while sitting for sculptor Augustus Saint-Gaudens. *(opposite)* Eleanor Roosevelt's activism did not appeal to everyone, but her admirers praised her for breaking old precedents about ladylike behavior. Here she visits servicemen abroad. *(above)*

**Stunned by attacks on her grammar and appearance, Rachel Jackson made it clear she never wanted to live in the White House.**

though they were running in tandem for a two-person job.

In at least one case, a wife's image may have contributed to her husband's defeat. Catherine ("Katie") Dunn Smith, whose husband, Alfred E. Smith, headed the Democratic ticket in 1928, was the convent-educated daughter of a successful New York contractor when she met and married the considerably less affluent Smith from the Lower East Side. As her husband moved up the political ladder, she dressed and behaved to suit herself.

Katie's natural good humor and casual ways, although emphatically endorsed by her husband, found many critics who saw her as "dowdy, vulgar, and unfit to be First Lady." Some opponents focused on the amount of jewelry she wore and her drinking habits, while others made fun of her New York accent and choice of words. One Texan, pointing out that Katie would be meeting foreign dignitaries if she got to the White House, asked, "Can you imagine? One of them might say, 'That's a nice hat,' and she'd say, 'You said a mouthful.'"

Attacks on Rachel Jackson exactly one hundred years earlier also centered on her lack of sophistication. Although she had grown up in a Tennessee family of substantial wealth, she had matured into a frontier woman of simple tastes and little regard for fashion. Her grammar, although no rougher than her husband's, was considered unsuitable for a "lady." In making fun of her rotund figure, critics snickered that her visit to New Orleans had resurrected an old French saying: "She shows how far the human skin can be stretched." Old rumors surfaced that the Jacksons had lived together before the divorce from her first husband became final, and although the stories were three decades old, they still hurt. Andrew Jackson blamed her critics for the heart attack that killed her shortly before his inauguration.

Since women had organized only on the local level in Rachel's time, no group was equipped to defend her, but by 1928, the situation had changed. Several prominent women, under the auspices of the

Democratic National Committee, spoke up for Katie Smith. Eleanor Roosevelt and journalist Ida Tarbell emphasized her humility and called her "a delightful homebody of retiring disposition, with unaffected good manners." In speeches to women's groups throughout the South, Frances Perkins, later to be named the first woman member of a president's cabinet, insisted that Katie was devoted to her family and never "touched a drop." Then in a final attempt to win audience approval, Perkins would conclude: "Anyhow, I tell you he loves her."

Al Smith lost the election of 1928 in a landslide for Herbert Hoover, but there is no way to measure the impact of rumors about his wife. A variety of other factors contributed to the Democrat's dismal showing. He was a Catholic in a largely Protestant nation, a "wet" on the

In 1928, when her husband ran for president, Catherine ("Katie") Smith (shown here with her husband and grandchildren) was criticized for wearing more jewelry than was currently fashionable.

Harry Truman did not take kindly to hints that his wife ought to look more glamorous.

Prohibition question, and his urban roots and accent soured many voters on him. A decade of prosperity gave Americans little reason to abandon Republican leaders who had led them through most of the 1920s. But Katie's lack of sophistication did not help her husband when women, who were her harshest critics, came out to vote in record numbers that year.

## Youthful, Slim Style

Sixty years later, a Republican candidate's wife faced a different kind of ridicule, and although it had little to do with her fitness to be First Lady, it called attention to her premature aging. Barbara Bush's hair first began turning gray when she was in her late twenties and she had used coloring to camouflage it, but by age sixty-three, when her husband was running for president, she had let it go snow white. The athletic figure of her youth had rounded out with the addition of a few pounds, and she had enough wrinkles, she sometimes joked, to make seersucker look smooth.

George Bush, although a year older than his wife, appeared at least a decade younger, leading to jokes about why a man would want to "marry his mother." The quips hurt, Barbara admitted, but she refused to alter her image. She had gamely offered to do all she could for her husband's career, except diet or dye her hair, and from the letters she received as First Lady, she concluded that "there were a lot of fat, wrinkled, white-haired ladies out there just tickled pink" with her stand.

Bess Truman had taken a similar tack. When Franklin Roosevelt's death suddenly elevated Harry to the presidency, Bess was sixty years old, one of the oldest to take on the job of First Lady. Although trim and athletic in her youth, she wore a matronly size sixteen "let out" by the time she got to the White House, and although she dieted when doctors told her to shed a few pounds for the sake of her health, she had no intention of serving as fashion plate for a youth-conscious nation.

Harry Truman emphatically approved her decision. When a male colleague quipped that "gentlemen prefer blondes," Harry countered that "real gentlemen prefer gray." Bess looked just "the way," he often said, "that a woman her age ought to look."

Few presidential wives have shown the self-confidence of Bess Truman and Barbara Bush. Most modern First Ladies have called in wardrobe consultants and made strong resolutions about losing pounds and looking more youthful. In her *White House Diary*, Lady Bird Johnson repeatedly promised herself to exercise more and reduce. The American public became so accustomed to candidates and their wives discussing

Because Barbara Bush and Nancy Reagan differed on the importance of fashion in their lives, reporters dubbed this photo "the War of the Plaids."

When she posed for this department store advertisement in 1839, Julia Gardiner (who later married President John Tyler) created a sensation in New York.

weight control (and vowing to lose pounds), that until her problem with Graves' disease was diagnosed, many people assumed that Barbara Bush's loss of nearly twenty pounds in 1989 resulted from a new regime.

Americans' fascination with slimness may partly explain why political wives have popularized rail-slim figures. Pat Nixon, who sometimes complained that so many parts of a political wife's life were beyond her control, watched her weight closely, and during her husband's two terms as vice president (1953–1961) she was frequently described as "painfully thin." Later, when they moved into the White House, Pat's small appetite caused comment among the staff.

Chief Usher J. B. West described how her first request threw the kitchen "into a tizzy." On the night of Richard Nixon's inauguration, the pantries were fully stocked and the staff waited confidently to fill any order that came down from upstairs. Word that the Nixons liked beef had preceded their arrival, and a good supply had been bought. But the kitchen was not prepared for Pat Nixon's order: the rest of the family would like steak in the upstairs dining room, but she wanted "a bowl of cottage cheese in my bedroom."

Not a spoonful of cottage cheese could be found in the White House, and a butler had to be dispatched by limousine to find a delicatessen open on that festive night. It was the last time, West later wrote, that the kitchen ran out of cottage cheese. He had worried because Mrs. Nixon was so thin, but now he realized, "She intended to stay that way."

Nancy Reagan, a size four, was the envy of American women who battled their entire lives to keep their dress sizes in the single digits, and Barbara Bush joked, with considerable exaggeration, that one of her thighs would just about fit in one of Mrs. Reagan's slim skirts. Both women had been plump youngsters, and Barbara Bush made jokes about it, saying that her mother told her skinny sister, "Eat, Martha—not you, Barbara." Nancy did not easily bare her thoughts on such personal matters, and photographs of her pre-Hollywood figure are scarce.

Trips to an Arizona spa helped Mamie Eisenhower trim pounds. Fifty-seven when she moved into the White House, she worked hard to appear younger. She spent so many mornings in bed that the domestic staff dubbed her "Sleeping Beauty," but the extended rest sustained a youthful enthusiasm, and she carefully chose clothes to reinforce the image. Resolutely rejecting "old lady" clothes and behavior, she asked her grandchildren to call her "Mimi" and wore strapless evening dresses with full skirts, much like those favored by high school seniors for their proms. Pink, her favorite color, appeared everywhere, even on her lipstick cases.

Youthfulness has always had many fans in America, and willingly or not, the youngest, most popular First Ladies have helped sell products. In the 1840s Julia Tyler became the toast of the capital, but a few years earlier she had created a scandal in New York society. Still in her teens, she had posed for a department store advertisement that referred to her as the "Rose of Long Island." At a time when a lady's name was supposed to appear in print only three times—at her birth, her marriage, and her death—modeling for advertisements was shocking behavior, and Julia's parents whisked her off for an extended stay in Europe.

Four decades later the next White House bride, twenty-two-year-old Frances Cleveland, found herself besieged with requests from advertisers to endorse their products. When she declined, they found ways to circumvent her and use her name and image anyway. Their gifts of perfume or soap guaranteed a thank-you note from Frances, and then the note could be published alongside her photo, giving the impression that she endorsed a particular scent or style.

One irate congressman decided that the unauthorized use of Frances's photo had to be stopped, and he introduced legislation banning it. But his colleagues recognized the futility of his attempt and refused to pass the measure. Presidents' wives, like other famous women, had to learn that they could not control all the uses of their name and image.

Mamie Eisenhower liked youthful clothes and had a special fondness for the color pink.

Americans continued to copy First Lady Cleveland, wearing their hair "à la Frances" and naming their baby girls for her.

In 1961 thirty-one-year-old Jacqueline Kennedy aroused similar admiration and emulation. Advertisers used models closely resembling her until the Better Business Bureau warned them to stop, and a Polish magazine proclaimed that she would likely "set the tone and style for the whole civilized world." Millions of women bought the straight, sleeveless dresses and pillbox hats that she popularized, teased their hair into bouffant styles, and chose the flat-heeled pumps that she preferred. Almost overnight, it seemed, the "Jackie" look replaced the full-skirted styles of the 1950s and Mamie bangs.

## Education

In their schooling, Jacqueline Kennedy and Mamie Eisenhower differed as much as in their styles. Mamie, thirty-three years older, had ended her formal education with finishing school, while Jacqueline earned a baccalaureate degree. Such a wide range was not unusual among First Ladies. Some ranked among the best schooled of their day, while others could barely read and write. Like other American women, their family circumstances mattered almost as much as the time in which they lived; even within a household, girls' education rarely equaled that of boys.

Abigail Adams (1797–1801) lamented that she never had a day of formal schooling in her life—but neither did most females of her time and social class. Her father, a congregational minister, possessed a large library that his three daughters freely used, and when Abigail's older sister married a man with scholarly interests, he included his bride's two younger sisters in his list of "charges." Long conversations with well-read women, including her grandmother Quincy, broadened Abigail's thinking beyond what might have been expected for a girl her age. When John Adams first met her, she was only fourteen, but the twenty-three-year-old Harvard graduate found her far from dull. He first mentioned

Bess Wallace Truman (first woman at left) earned a reputation as an excellent tennis player in her youth.

her in his diary as "a wit," and their courtship letters contain many literary references.

White House women rarely cultivate an image as intellectuals, but Lou Hoover certainly qualified as erudite. She could boast—although that would not have been her style—that she was the first presidential wife to hold the same college degree as her husband, in the same field (geology) and from the same university. Although a few months older than Herbert, she took longer than he to decide what she wanted to do with her life, probably because so few of the options open to females in

Lou Henry Hoover spoke several languages and translated (with her husband) a mining text from the Latin. *(above)* Lou's travels with her husband and sons took her all over the world. *(opposite)*

the 1890s appealed to her.

After graduating from high school at age sixteen, Lou studied for three years in California normal (teacher training) schools, but then hesitated to use her teaching certificate. After short stints as a bank teller and substitute teacher, she enrolled at the newly founded Stanford University to study geology—a field in which women rarely ventured.

At Stanford, Lou met a twenty-year-old teaching assistant who was as serious about geology as she, and very soon, Herbert Hoover and Lou were spending their spare time together. When he graduated first and set off for Australia to make his name (and a sizable personal fortune) in mining, she stayed behind to finish her degree. His telegraphed marriage proposal a year later was accepted immediately, beginning what turned out to be a particularly companionable marriage that lasted until her death in 1944.

In many ways, their marriage extended Lou's education because her husband's jobs took them all over the world. In China, where they arrived just as the Boxer Rebellion broke out, Lou cycled between bullets, played solitaire while fighting continued on her doorstep, learned to speak and read Mandarin, and began what turned into a valuable collection of blue porcelain vases of the Ming dynasty period. When Bert traveled to Korea, Japan, Burma, and Russia, she went along, packing their two young sons in a basket on her back. While they were living in London, she and her husband worked together translating an obscure mining book from sixteenth-century Latin. When it was published privately in 1912, with both Hoovers listed as translators, it won the Mining and Metallurgical Society's gold award.

Another intellectual First Lady, Sarah Polk, also associated her name with ideas and books, although in her time, college education was not available to women. In 1820, when she was of an age to enroll, not one college in the nation admitted women. (None would attempt coeducation until 1833, when Sarah was already the wife of a congressman, and

Before Lucy Webb married Rutherford Hayes, she graduated from the Wesleyan Female Academy in Cincinnati, Ohio. Here she is shown (center) with two friends.

the first women's college was established after she left the White House.) Sarah was first tutored at home, then attended school in Nashville, and at age thirteen went off to Salem Female Academy in North Carolina. Considered one of the best schools for girls, the academy had a reputation that reached Tennessee, and Sarah and her younger sister rode two hundred miles on horseback to enroll. In addition to the usual subjects that all girls were expected to master—needlepoint, music, and household management—she took academic subjects that other schools reserved for boys.

Sarah's studies ended abruptly when her father died and she was called home, but her intellectual curiosity remained for life. In the White House, she made a point of inviting writers and of reading their work before she met them. When questioned about where she found the time to prepare so thoroughly for her visitors, she explained, "I could not be so unkind as to appear wholly ignorant and unmindful" of an author's work. She cultivated friendships with some of Washington's most forceful women and powerful men, and they rewarded her with many compliments. Supreme Court Justice Joseph Story took the unusual step of publishing a poem in her honor—it suggested Sarah lacked none of the qualities deemed desirable in a woman: "For I have listened to thy voice / and watched thy playful mind / Truth in its noblest sense thy choice / Yet gentle, graceful, kind."

The equally popular Dolley Madison had less formal schooling than Sarah Polk, but she is not known to have complained. Born to Quakers, who permitted more equality between the sexes than did most Protestant denominations, Dolley was educated alongside her brothers in the family's small shop, where she learned rudimentary reading and arithmetic. Though she showed little acquaintance with the classics, her respect for books was obvious and she frequently carried one at White House receptions, explaining that if she had trouble engaging a guest in conversation, she could always fall back on the volume in her hand.

Other nineteenth-century First Ladies pushed at the boundaries of women's education but never quite equaled the schooling their brothers got. Lucy Hayes (1877–1881), sometimes singled out as the first president's wife to have a college degree, actually graduated from Wesleyan Female College in Cincinnati. The four-hundred-woman student body followed a rigorous curriculum, including geometry, geology, and astronomy, but it could not compare with that of Ohio Wesleyan University, where Lucy's two older brothers studied. Lucy's widowed mother had moved to Delaware, Ohio, for the express purpose of enrolling her two sons in the newly founded Ohio Wesleyan, but she sent Lucy to a girls' school in Cincinnati.

Lucretia Garfield (1881) started out on the same education track as her husband but their paths soon split. Both enrolled at the Ohio Eclectic Institute (later renamed Hiram College), but when he transferred to the more prestigious Williams College in Massachusetts, she remained at the institute. Although she compiled an outstanding record and became an eloquent public speaker, she found teaching school the only job open to her, while James Garfield quickly became the president of a teachers' college, entered politics, and was admitted to the bar.

Not until the 1920s would the United States have a First Lady who held a baccalaureate degree from a university. Grace Goodhue Coolidge had enrolled at the University of Vermont with the class of 1901 and remembered little controversy on the subject: "There was no discussion about my going to college," she said, "although the percentage of women students was small then." She sang in the glee club and served as vice president of her class but played down her popularity. After becoming a national figure, this perceptive woman wrote, "When I can no longer speak for myself, I hope nobody will attempt to show that I was one of the most popular girls in the college . . . I was not . . . but I had many unusual friends whose loyalty has stood the test of the years."

As a young girl, Grace had decided to teach the hard of hearing, and

Ellen Wilson, an accomplished painter before she became First Lady, had little time for art in the White House. *(above)* Her *Autumn Day* was exhibited in the annual exhibition at the Pennsylvania Academy of Fine Arts while she was First Lady. *(below)*

after earning her B.A., she went on to the renowned Clarke Institute in Massachusetts. Since Clarke did not encourage sign language, she learned to help hearing-impaired people form the sounds that other people used and to "hear" by touching faces and vocal cords. Later, Grace's choice of career inspired many jokes, especially in regard to her husband's famous taciturnity. A White House visitor, dismayed by the president's lack of interest in making small talk, commented, "If Mrs. Coolidge could teach the deaf to talk, why couldn't she teach Cal?" (Known as the most laconic of all presidents, Calvin Coolidge reportedly nonplussed a White House dinner guest who confessed to having wagered that she could get him to say "more than two words." He responded, "You lose.")

Although Grace Coolidge's training made her one of the first White House wives equipped for a professional career, several of her predecessors had prepared for the possibility that they would have to earn a living, and three of them had chosen the arts. Florence Harding (1921–1923) attended the Cincinnati Conservatory, gave piano lessons in Marion, Ohio, and continued to set aside an hour for practice each day, even in the White House. Earlier, Caroline Harrison (1889–1892) had studied at the Miami (Ohio) Conservatory and taught music in Kentucky. Just before she got to the White House, Ellen Axson Wilson (1913–1914) had exhibited her paintings in juried shows, sometimes under an assumed name that concealed her connection to Woodrow.

But most of the First Ladies who had worked had been teachers, which was until the twentieth century almost the only career open to respectable middle-class women (from whose ranks most presidential wives came). Eight of the first thirty-eight taught in some kind of school (including one law school). Others taught privately. It was so widely assumed that any president's wife who had earned money outside the home or family business had taught that when Bess Truman moved into the White House in April 1945, newspapers mistakenly reported

As a Congressman's wife, Lady Bird Johnson enjoyed showing her husband's constituents around Washington. *(above)* Grace Coolidge, who had trained to teach the hearing-impaired, "talked" with Helen Keller. *(opposite)*

Jacqueline Bouvier (later Kennedy), at left, took her first job as "inquiring photographer" with the *Washington Times Herald. (above)* At the time of her marriage in 1905, Eleanor Roosevelt showed few of the traits that would later mark her as an extraordinary First Lady. *(opposite)*

that she had been a teacher. Her three immediate predecessors—Eleanor Roosevelt, Lou Hoover, and Grace Coolidge—had indeed been teachers.

As a young woman, Eleanor Roosevelt began teaching dance at a settlement house in New York's Lower East Side, but she quit when her mother-in-law objected that she might bring home diseases. Later, after her own children were grown, Eleanor taught history at Todhunter, a private girls' school that she and her friends ran on New York's Upper

When students objected that she was not qualified, Barbara Bush (at right) invited Raisa Gorbachev, university professor and wife of the president of the Soviet Union, to accompany her and speak at Wellesley's commencement.

East Side. Helping her young charges explore new ideas pleased her more "than anything I have ever done," she sometimes said, and while Franklin was governor, she determinedly commuted from Albany to Manhattan to teach. In 1933, when she faced the burdens of being the nation's First Lady, she reluctantly turned in her resignation.

Whether presidents' wives influenced other women to enter teaching is difficult to judge, since their time in the schoolroom preceded their White House days. It is more likely that in their youth First Ladies had simply responded to the same opportunities that shaped all women's lives. Until about 1950, teaching jobs rarely required a college degree, and many middle-class women used the job as a way to get out of their parents' home and establish social and financial independence before

they married and set up their own homes.

Teaching continued to attract twentieth-century women. Pat Nixon (born 1912), who needed to support herself after her parents died, taught high school and advised the cheerleaders. Lady Bird Johnson (also born 1912) faced no immediate financial need, but dreaming of a career in some "faraway place," she had decided that a journalism degree or a teacher's certificate would help her get there. Lyndon came along before she had the chance to try, and she settled for a full-time job as a busy politician's wife.

Not until the 1990s would Americans get a presidential spouse with a professional degree identical to her husband's, but Hillary Rodham Clinton's breaking of precedent resulted partly from changes in the

Mamie Eisenhower wore fashionable anklets and heels as she posed with her husband and dog in San Remo, Italy, in the 1920s.

nation. Even she made this point. When a television interviewer asked her to explain how her experiences as attorney would alter the First Lady role, she replied: "What I represent is generational change. It's not about me."

Hillary (born in 1947) thus acknowledged a remarkable shift in the generation that separated her from her predecessor, Barbara Bush (born in 1925). The younger woman not only graduated from college, but completed law school and worked as a professional throughout her adult life. Barbara had dropped out of college after one year to get married. She never held a full-time job, centering her entire life around her husband's career and her four children. When Hillary, a successful attorney, gave birth to her only child, she returned to work almost immediately. The contrast between them is underlined by their names. While most Americans would have trouble remembering the maiden name of Barbara (Pierce) Bush, few forget that Hillary was born and lived much of her adult life as a Rodham.

Both women are typical of their times. A working mother in a two-parent household would have been unusual in 1952, when Barbara's oldest child entered school, but by the time Chelsea Clinton was born in 1979, more than half the mothers of preschool children held jobs outside the home. That would have been unthinkable to Mamie Eisenhower, who joked, when someone suggested that she write her memoirs, that she did not like to work.

Mamie actually marks a turning point. The last White House wife to be born in the nineteenth century, she apparently never considered attending college. All but one of her successors enrolled in college at least for a while, and the one exception, Betty Ford, often said she regretted that she had not.

Betty's formal education ended when she decided to leave Michigan to study modern dance in New York with the pioneering choreographer Martha Graham. Unable to make a living in dance, Betty modeled

Hillary Rodham (second from left) was selected by other students to speak at Wellesley's commencement in 1969. The main speaker, Senator Edward Brook, is at the far right.

This engraving of the young Martha Washington gives little hint of the independence for which she is credited. *(above)* Barbara Pierce married George Bush when she was nineteen, making her one of only three First Ladies who had been teenage brides. (The others were Eliza Johnson and Rosalynn Carter.) *(opposite)*

clothes, and later, when she returned to Grand Rapids, she turned her fashion sense into a job as a buyer at a local department store. After a brief first marriage ending in divorce, she wed aspiring politician Gerald Ford in 1948 and immediately quit her job, thus conforming to the pattern of most of her contemporaries.

## Marriage Patterns

In choosing Gerald Ford, Betty is one of very few First Ladies who did not "marry down" (although she may have wondered what kind of husband she was getting when he arrived late for the ceremony, his shoes still caked with mud from giving a campaign speech on damp turf). Most presidents' wives have come from families considerably above their husbands' socially and financially.

Sometimes the differences were remarkable. When Martha Parke Custis's husband died, he left her what would be in twentieth-century dollars a multimillion-dollar estate. George Washington's family, although of substantial wealth, possessed far less than Martha when the two met and married in 1759.

Abigail Adams's father had little use for John, even though he had a Harvard degree and practiced law. Eighteenth-century Massachusetts was producing a glut of lawyers, and few of them could expect to match the earnings of Abigail's father, the Reverend William Smith. When the bride's father performed the ceremony, he took as his text a verse from the book of Luke: "John came neither eating bread nor drinking wine and some say he has a devil in him." The bridegroom took the text in stride, perhaps in jest, and boasted to a friend that he had married into the family of the "richest clergyman in the province."

Simple fortune hunting hardly explains these matches or many others. In two of the cases, the bride's family had lost its wealth by the time the weddings took place. Elizabeth Kortright Monroe's parents had sided with the Loyalists in the American Revolution and sacrificed most of

Anna Symmes Harrison declined to attend her husband's 1841 inauguration, and before she could travel to Washington, he died.

their personal holdings to a lost cause. Louisa Johnson Adams's father, a merchant from Baltimore, lost a business empire in London just weeks before her marriage to John Quincy Adams.

Both women brought social skills and contacts that may have helped their husbands, but Louisa remained convinced she had contributed little. Her family's diminished circumstances remained a lifelong shame. A quarter century later she was still explaining to her children that a substantial wedding gift from her parents had never materialized and that John Quincy had married into a "ruined house."

Louisa's foreign birth, more than her small inheritance, figured in the uncongenial reception she got from many Americans, including her in-laws. After growing up in France and England, Louisa felt strange and out-of-place when, at age twenty-six, she first landed in Boston. She pronounced herself "utterly astonished" by the cool welcome she received. Mother-in-law Abigail Adams never did warm to Louisa.

While it is fairly obvious why men would wish to marry up, thus gaining the advantages that their wives' social skills and money would bring, the women's motivation is not so clear. Since most of the women had other choices, they must have spotted ambition or a potential for achievement that others missed. For some, like Florence Harding, the marriage opened a back door into politics in a time when women rarely ran for office or got involved in campaigns. Her father failed to perceive much promise in Warren and refused to speak to his daughter for seven years after the marriage.

Other First Ladies married despite loud objections from their parents. Anna Symmes waited for her father to leave town before she called in a justice of the peace to perform her marriage to the young William Henry Harrison. Julia Dent's prosperous parents thought she could do better than tie her future to a man who showed as little potential as Ulysses S. Grant. He had graduated from West Point but had excelled only in horseback riding. Socially prominent Madge Wallace made no secret of the fact that she thought her only daughter, Bess, could do better than marry a farmer named Harry S Truman.

## Changing Roles for Women

Hillary Rodham Clinton's baby boom generation married later than had been the pattern in the United States. Refusing to compete among themselves to see who would be the first to put a "Mrs." in her name, some preferred to be known as "Ms." even after they married, and many wanted to keep their own family names. Hillary married in 1975, but not until 1982, after Arkansas voters objected during Bill's unsuccessful bid for reelection to governor, did she tack "Clinton" onto her name. Even then, she continued to use Rodham professionally.

Several presidents' wives helped raise the number of women appointed to high office, although some refused to claim credit. Lou Hoover remained resolutely silent on the subject, but her husband set a record in appointing women to jobs that require Senate approval. In his four-year term, he named seven, bringing the total up to twenty, double what it had been in 1920. Eleanor Roosevelt drew upon her large network of competent professional women to suggest candidates for jobs in social service and related fields, and it is not insignificant that Franklin Roosevelt named two women as ambassadors—thus breaking an old, strong barrier against them in the diplomatic arena.

Later First Ladies were more candid about their impact. Rosalynn Carter's husband never got the opportunity to nominate a justice for the U.S. Supreme Court, "but it was always understood between us," she wrote, "that a woman would be appointed if a vacancy occurred." Betty Ford admitted that she tried unsuccessfully to add a woman to the Republican national ticket in 1976.

The pool of qualified women had grown much larger by 1993. Law schools and medical schools were graduating nearly as many females as males, and women earned more than half of the doctorates in the social

Betty Ford used her training in dance when she met young people in China.

sciences. Hillary Rodham Clinton, after years of legal work and volunteer efforts with the Children's Defense Fund and the Legal Services Corporation, could reach out to her colleagues for names of qualified women. When President Clinton began filling jobs, it was widely rumored that Hillary helped, and insiders spoke of "Hillary's Friends" as a category of candidates separate from "Bill's Friends." Donna Shalala, secretary of health and human services, and Janet Reno, attorney general, were only two of the high-level appointments, both women and men, believed to come from the First Lady's list.

The apparent enthusiasm with which First Ladies pushed their sisters forward had not been predicted. Some observers, persuaded by a few nineteenth-century examples, argued that White House women would jealously protect their access to power and resent competition for the limelight. Mary Lincoln and Ida McKinley, who did not have good relationships with other women, had verbally attacked those they perceived as competing with them. On one occasion, Ida accused a female guest of wanting "to be in my place." Her outburst was probably the cry of a troubled woman, but it raised questions about how presidents' wives would regard women who held power in their own right.

Such suspicions no doubt prompted reporters to question Betty Ford and Rosalynn Carter at a conference in Grand Rapids, Michigan, in 1984, the year that Democrats nominated Geraldine Ferraro to run on a national ticket headed by Walter Mondale. When asked how a First Lady would relate to a woman vice president, both had seemed uncertain how to answer. Although their hesitation may have resulted from their uncertainties about the political effects of any comment, some members of the audience incorrectly interpreted their reticence as disapproval.

Some tension between political wives and women candidates may survive (as does the tension between achieving women and the population as a whole), and it possibly prompted Barbara Bush's comment on

Geraldine Ferraro in 1984. Barbara's husband had the same place on the Republican ticket that year as Ferraro did on the Democratic, and among the heavy campaign coverage were several stories on the wealth of the two families—with each candidate claiming the more modest ground. When asked her opinion of her husband's counterpart, Barbara Bush answered (off the record, she thought) that "I can't say it, but it rhymes with rich." When the comment was published, she tried to cover up, saying she had meant "witch" rather than the derogatory term for strong women that most people thought she had intended.

## Clothing: Fashion and Cost

Whether elected in their own right or standing by their men, women in politics find inordinate attention directed to what they wear. A man might put on the same suit every day without finding himself ridiculed in the press, but a woman is not permitted the same freedom. Presidential wives have, since the beginning of the Republic, found themselves criticized and ridiculed because of what they chose to wear.

Nothing too risky is wise, as Grace Coolidge found out when culottes briefly became fashionable in the 1920s. Her husband, though frugal, took great interest in her outfits (and appeared disappointed if she donned the same party dress twice), and he did not want to see her in culottes. When she purchased a pair, he suggested she return them because "no woman in the family ever wore them." And she did.

Nancy Reagan ran into similar trouble with high-fashion pants. When she and the president hosted a dinner in Paris in 1982, she drew considerable comment for her black satin tunic and knickers outfit designed by Galanos. Official guests, dressed more conservatively, were surprised rather than critical, but one American fashion editor described the outfit scathingly: "The tunic had all the style of a maternity top and the knickers made her calves look bloated." Nancy never wore it again.

No First Lady dared wear pants in the nineteenth century, although

Nancy Reagan wore a knickers outfit designed by Galanos when she greeted French President and Madame Mitterrand at dinner in Paris.

Eleanor Roosevelt sometimes wore her riding habit to greet guests. *(above)* Even as a young flapper, Mamie Eisenhower took great interest in clothes. *(opposite)*

many feminist reformers considered them a healthful change from the tight corsets, cumbersome hoops, and bustles that hampered both breathing and movement. Around midcentury, a movement started to substitute Amelia Bloomer's loose baggy pants outfits. "Bloomers" found support among women who fought for the right to vote, go to college, and own property in their own names after marriage, but they never caught on with the public at large.

In the 1930s, slacks and pants did move into mainstream America, but presidents' wives remained wary of them, avoiding cameras when wearing them. Photographs are rare before the 1970s. Pat Nixon wore slacks in private, but when she agreed to model them for *McCall's* magazine, her decision was attributed to an attempt to remake her image.

Eleanor Roosevelt sometimes received reporters while clad in riding clothes, but she probably never considered that she was making a statement. Her interest in fashion was slight, and she sometimes bought dresses "in the ten-dollar range," according to her secretary, although her income, both inherited and earned, would have provided for any extravagance. Eleanor may have taken a lesson from her aunt Edith, who lived in the White House thirty-two years earlier, before fashionable ready-made clothes were widely available and when most middle-class women went to a dressmaker. Theodore Roosevelt's wife relegated her wardrobes to little importance and took pride in remodeling outfits from previous years. When a newspaper columnist speculated in print that the First Lady had spent less than three hundred dollars a year on her wardrobe, Edith Roosevelt proudly clipped the article for her scrapbook.

Ellen Wilson, Woodrow's first wife, proved herself just as frugal but less confident. When her husband was president of Princeton University and governor of New Jersey, she had kept a small wardrobe suitable for the few public occasions she faced during the year, but she understood that in the White House she would make more appearances and get con-

Glamorous Jacqueline Kennedy inspired many imitators.

siderably more attention. Since she had to pay for all her purchases out of her own pocket, she carefully ordered a few new things and then arranged to have other garments altered and updated. When newspapers reported that she had splurged on seven gowns costing between $200 and $300 each, she produced receipts for her entire wardrobe, totaling $140.84—including materials for repairing old garments.

By the second half of the twentieth century, fashion was a major American industry and designers had learned the value a president's wife could have for their business. Jacqueline Kennedy helped make Oleg Cassini a household word. Subsequently, other First Ladies like Barbara Bush drew attention to their favorite designers and fashions. When Hillary Rodham Clinton was photographed in a designer dress, the original model sold well and, like Jacqueline Kennedy's dresses, stimulated copies that sold in the thousands.

Hillary's appearance in a fashion layout in *Vogue* magazine brought criticism as well as praise. Some readers found it refreshing that a woman reportedly cerebral and policy-conscious could care about what she wore; others thought she sent the wrong message to young girls. One irate mother wrote to her local newspaper, "She didn't prove, as her advocates insist, that a modern woman can be all things. She proved that after becoming a powerful lawyer and policy maker, she still needed to be a sex object."

Nancy Reagan drew different criticism. When she agreed to wear the clothes of various American designers, they obligingly supplied complimentary outfits for her. She defended the loans, saying she was boosting her nation's fashion industry, but voters disagreed. Her advisers negotiated a truce: Nancy would stop wearing borrowed clothes and return those she had already accepted or turn them over to museums. The First Lady made light of the whole discussion, and at the annual Gridiron dinner she delighted guests by singing about giving her "Secondhand clothes / To museum collections and traveling shows."

## Smoking and Drinking

Even personal choices a First Lady makes about smoking and drinking make national news, and some White House residents tailor their public images to appeal to voters. Jacqueline Kennedy, although reportedly a heavy smoker, was rarely photographed with a cigarette in her hand, and pictures showing her with a cigarette were closed to researchers at the Kennedy Library for many years.

Smoking among White House women has had a long, erratic history. Rachel Jackson was known to enjoy a pipe, as did most frontier women of her time, and this was held against her when her husband ran for president. One of her successors, Margaret Taylor (1849–1850), seems

Nancy Reagan amused reporters by appearing in this garb and singing about wearing secondhand clothes.

Just days before her son Patrick was born (and before the connection between smoking and low-weight babies was clear) Jacqueline Kennedy relaxed with a cigarette.

to have been falsely accused. Margaret grew up in the East and attended one of the more fashionable girls' schools in Manhattan before marrying Zachary Taylor, a military man who took her to the frontier. She apparently had little liking for the limelight, and when he won the presidency, she stayed upstairs at the White House, sending her married daughter down to greet guests. Because of her reclusiveness, rumors circulated that she was a dull sort who could barely converse beyond "a moan" and contented herself with puffing away on a pipe. Taylor family records suggest quite a different woman, and her grandson insisted that her aversion to smoke was so well-known that no one dared light up in her presence.

Victorian standards of the late nineteenth century placed large barriers between the sexes, and smoking was deemed proper only for men. By the 1920s, when advertising geniuses, such as George Washington

Hill, looked for a way to increase the sale of cigarettes, they concentrated on the female market. Hill ran a Lucky Strike advertisement with the homey caption "It's Toasted," and a subsequent commercial showed a woman seated on a sofa beside a man who's smoking, while she says, "Blow some my way."

World War I and the decade that followed encouraged other fractures in the dividers between the sexes. Although Prohibition remained the law, many Americans determined to imbibe anyway, and the "speakeasies" that sprang up in major cities served both sexes. Women entered marathon dance contests, bobbed their hair, discarded their corsets, and shortened their skirts.

A cigarette added a touch of sophistication, and several First Ladies counted themselves among the converted, but since not everyone approved, they exercised caution. Grace Coolidge confined her smoking to private places and permitted no photographs of herself holding a cigarette. Florence Harding went even farther—she did not wish to be photographed alongside a woman who appeared to be smoking, and during one picture-taking session she abruptly knocked the offending article from the mouth of her friend Evalyn MacLean.

Eleanor Roosevelt, very much a product of Victorian times, at first put cigarettes and alcohol on her list of "fast" behavior, permitted for men but not for women. After her marriage, she watched Franklin party into the morning hours but usually got herself to bed early. In one oft repeated story, she left a party ahead of him, then found she did not have her house key. Rather than go back and interrupt his fun, she sat sleeping on the steps of their home until he returned several hours later.

By the 1930s, Eleanor's self-confidence had grown and she had moved beyond such martyrdom. Her women friends insisted that distinctions between the sexes should be eliminated, and as First Lady she did her part to help them in many areas, including the matter of smoking. Cigarettes were passed to both men and women after White House dinners, and Eleanor herself lit up on some occasions just to show which side she was on.

Americans' continued disapproval of smoking by their First Ladies is underlined by their reactions to it and by the lengths to which presidents' wives go to conceal their cigarettes. When Pat Nixon smoked after dinner in a Washington restaurant in 1973, the *New York Times* carried a story about it, along with her press secretary's assurance that "she probably does not inhale." The fuss was remarkable considering that at the time Golda Meir, prime minister of Israel, was frequently photographed holding a cigarette.

Consumption of alcoholic beverages by First Ladies was equally subject to scrutiny, especially after 1850. The first presidential wives routinely included rum among the beverages served at political events, but the strong temperance movement in the late nineteenth century led to a change. For many Americans, abstinence became the ideal, and imbibing even a drop of alcohol was considered excessive, the equivalent of drunkenness. After Lucy Hayes showed how valuable a temperance stand could be in winning votes, her successors were tempted to follow suit. Young Frances Cleveland toasted at her own wedding reception with mineral water and routinely turned her wine goblets upside-down at state dinners to signal her stand on temperance.

Lucretia Garfield considered the fuss unreasonable, and when a temperance advocate appealed to her to continue Lucy Hayes's ban, she refused. "Drinking wine at a respectable dinner" had "little to do with drunkenness," Lucretia wrote, and she did not approve of giving the subject "so much importance."

Despite the eventual collapse of the temperance movement and the failure of Prohibition, modern First Ladies made a point of concealing their drinking, even if they confined it to small amounts in social settings. Reporter Helen Thomas pointed out that Jacqueline Kennedy would let the drinks tray pass, untouched, rather than risk being photographed with a glass in hand. When newspaper stories about Bess Truman implied that she did not drink, she let them go uncorrected, though White House staff later set the record straight. Chief Usher J. B. West recalled how Mrs. Truman had rung for the steward on her first evening at 1600 Pennsylvania Avenue and ordered old-fashioneds for herself and the president. The bartender, who prided himself on his mixing skill, prepared the drinks and took them in. Bess made no comment except to pronounce her drink "too sweet." A similar order the following evening produced a similar response. Finally, an exasperated steward poured straight bourbon over ice, and this time the First Lady smiled approvingly. "This," she said, "is how we like our old-fashioneds."

## Adventuring

First Ladies serve as models in many areas, and their decisions can influence an industry and change minds about what is safe or acceptable behavior. In the 1930s, when air travel was still considered risky and many Americans refused to try it, airlines attempted various inducements, including hiring nurses in uniform to travel as "flight attendants." But their best advertisement came unsolicited from Eleanor Roosevelt, who published an article, "Flying Is Fun," and routinely flew between New York and Washington. Photographed alongside planes and interviewed inside them, she conferred an invaluable seal of approval on air travel. Airline officials gratefully pronounced her their best friend since Charles Lindbergh. "The Flying First Lady" even accepted an invitation from Amelia Earhart to fly with her over the capital at night—the pilot wearing a long evening dress as she sat at the controls.

A few decades earlier, when the automobile carried similar connotations of risk and daring, another First Lady helped change minds about its safety. Even before she married Woodrow Wilson, Edith Galt had already made a name for herself around Washington, where she had a jewelry store near the White House. She became the first woman to

Eleanor Roosevelt was sometimes called the "Flying First Lady" because of the number of flights she took between the capital and New York.

Edith Galt Wilson happily drove herself around the capital before she became First Lady.

drive herself around in an electric auto, and traffic officers learned to recognize her and obligingly wave her through red lights.

Not all Edith's successors boasted her prowess at the wheel; some preferred leaving the driving to others. Florence Harding, who liked to ride horses and determinedly sat astride while most women rode sidesaddle, balked at operating powered vehicles. One of her critics suggested that the automobile was the only part of Warren's life that she did not try to run.

Lou Hoover liked to drive, perhaps more than she should have, because she reportedly liked to speed. A major newspaper announced that she was giving up driving one winter—without mentioning why—but friends were not convinced. Those who accompanied her to

Rapidan, the country retreat the Hoovers created sixty-five miles east of Washington, told how she would sometimes leave the White House in a chauffeured limousine, then stop outside the city limits and change cars. Taking over the wheel of a roadster, she would be out of sight before anyone realized the switch had occurred.

Eleanor Roosevelt's driving record also caused some difficulties, although she relished the freedom she felt behind the wheel. Traveling incognito, she escaped the duties associated with her national prominence and relaxed in the security of being a private person. "I drove up in the capacity of ER," she wrote about one trip, "and only on arriving became FDR's wife." But Eleanor's children considered her reckless at the wheel. Her most publicized accident occurred when she knocked down the stone gatepost at the Hyde Park estate. Her mother-in-law, who left the maneuvering of automobiles to others, simply pursed her lips when informed of the mishap and refused to comment.

After World War II, security arrangements for chief executives and their wives restricted them from driving themselves, and by the 1990s, it was rare for a First Lady to be photographed at the wheel on public roads. But whatever hobby or activity she takes up, she is likely to influence a lot of Americans to do likewise.

## Sickness and Health

Illness at the White House can send thousands of Americans to their physicians, and how the president and his wife convalesce affects public behavior also. A First Lady who takes to her bed for months after a minor illness sends one message about what is necessary or appropriate; one who resumes her activities as soon as possible sends another. Mid-nineteenth-century presidential wives typically endorsed the contemporary view that a fainting, neurasthenic woman was attractive. A long list, including Anna Harrison (1841), Letitia Tyler (1841–1842), Margaret Taylor (1849–1850), Abigail Fillmore (1850–1853), and Jane Pierce

On camping trips in her youth, Lady Bird Johnson had a reputation for taking risks.

Eliza Johnson, ill with tuberculosis, appeared in public only twice while her husband was president.

(1853–1857), retired to their rooms, leaving the First Lady work to others. While some of them were indeed seriously ill, others may have been responding to middle- and upper-class ideas that "ladies" were delicate creatures, often ill.

Eliza Johnson (1865–1869) illustrates the pattern as well as anyone. When Andrew Johnson became president after Abraham Lincoln was assassinated, Eliza was fifty-five years old and probably tubercular. She attended only one White House dinner during the entire four years that he served and coughed herself to the door a few minutes after being seated. Her only other official appearance as First Lady came at a party she gave for her grandchildren, and this time she excused herself from her young guests, saying, "You see, I am an invalid."

The severity of Eliza's illness is unclear, however. She regularly read newspapers, clipping those parts that she thought her husband most needed to see, and she welcomed daily visits with her young grandchildren as much as they delighted in seeing her. After leaving the White House, she returned to Tennessee and was well enough when Andrew Johnson died in 1871 to be appointed his executrix.

In the twentieth century, when definitions of femininity relied less on weakness and helplessness, these retreats into invalidism became less common. Modern First Ladies have played down their illnesses. When Nancy Reagan learned she had breast cancer in October 1987, she wrote in her diary, "I have to keep up my schedule," and she did. Given the choice between a radical mastectomy and more limited surgery followed by radiation treatments, she opted for the first, saying, "In my job, there is no way" to schedule radiation.

In the ten days she had to wait before undergoing surgery, Nancy worried—but she also completed a list of activities that gave no hint of illness. She made two trips out of town: one to Chicago to receive an award and the other (on the day before her operation) to New Hampshire to meet leaders of the Foster Grandparents Program. In

Washington, she conferred on White House repairs, made plans for the Drug Abuse Foundation, worked on her book, and hosted a state dinner for the president of El Salvador. Until she entered the hospital, she kept her medical news out of the press.

Just before surgery, Nancy joked with her doctors, saying the operation would go quickly: "Dolly Parton I'm not." But ten days later, after being released from the hospital, she received another shock when her mother died of a stroke. Instead of concentrating on convalescing, Nancy

**Nancy Reagan returned to a festive White House after her surgery for cancer.**

Betty Ford earned a reputation as one of the most candid of all First Ladies.

flew to Arizona and handled arrangements for the funeral. A week later she was back in the White House, planning state dinners for the leaders of the Soviet Union and Israel.

Betty Ford had been equally upbeat and determined about her mastectomy in 1974. Against advice that such topics should not be discussed publicly, she and her family released all the details. As a result, television and the press featured discussions of breast cancer (previously considered almost unmentionable) and physicians debated the merits of radical vs. more limited surgery. Talk about the importance of early detection persuaded many women to schedule mammograms, and doctors reported a tenfold increase in the number of women seeking examinations.

The public discussion of Betty Ford's health was remarkable. Only two decades earlier, Mamie Eisenhower had refused to confirm that she had undergone a hysterectomy. The word "hysterectomy" did not appear in the White House press release, which said only that the First Lady had undergone "a two-hour operation by a gynecologist similar to those that many women undergo in middle age." When a reporter inquired if that had been a hysterectomy, the press secretary replied that he "could not go beyond the original statement."

Betty Ford and Nancy Reagan both concentrated on the value of being open and honest. Nancy took heart from the fact that the woman who fitted her for a prosthesis reported an upswing in business, and Betty focused on the lives she had helped save. "Lying in the hospital," she wrote, "I'd come to recognize more clearly the power of the woman in the White House . . . a power which could be used to help."

Such candor would have been incomprehensible in the nineteenth century when First Ladies refused to reveal what ailed them. One of the sickliest, Ida Saxton McKinley, was known in her youth as vigorous and headstrong. After a trip to Europe, she took a job in her father's bank—an unusual occupation for a woman at the time—and worked there until her marriage. But her entire personality changed after her two young

Barbara Bush did not let Graves' disease put a dent in a busy White House schedule that included frequent visits from grandchildren.

daughters died in the 1870s. Every ounce of good health and good humor seemed squeezed from her, and she spent the remainder of her years a sickly, bad-tempered woman.

Among her maladies was a form of epilepsy, although neither she nor her husband acknowledged it. Epilepsy was still so misunderstood in the 1890s that the word rarely appeared in print, and one of Ida's nieces later admitted that she had not known its meaning. When an opposition newspaper speculated that the First Lady was epileptic, the niece assumed it was some derogatory term that politicians used to discredit

**Ida McKinley's epileptic seizures became the subject of considerable talk while she was First Lady.**

opponents, not a health problem.

In William McKinley's two decades of government service, Ida became a public figure and the subject of many rumors. Her devoted husband altered seating arrangements at official dinners so he could sit next to her, ready to take charge if she needed assistance. One White House guest told how Ida had begun shaking violently during one dinner, and without missing a beat in the conversation, the president threw his large white handkerchief over her head and continued talking. Later, when the seizure had ended, Ida removed the cover and resumed her part in the discussion.

Very quickly, styles of convalescence shifted in the White House, and twentieth-century First Ladies concentrated on speedy recoveries. When Helen Taft suffered a stroke in early 1909, she dedicated the summer to regaining the ability to form sounds. By October of that year, she was back in the capital. Although her daughter and sister substituted for her when a lengthy speech was required, she gamely tried to fulfill other duties.

Florence Harding also worked hard to appear healthier than she was, and she had considerable experience in concealment. Older than her husband by seven years, she relied on camouflage to appear younger. Rouging her cheeks to approximate the glow of youth, she favored wide velvet bands to cover neck wrinkles. An even bigger concern than age, but one that Florence kept strictly to herself, was her health. A serious kidney ailment showed up in her persistently swollen ankles, and fatigue sometimes kept her in bed half the day, especially when she faced the prospect of standing in a receiving line or hosting a party likely to run into the late evening hours. But "the duchess," as her husband always called her, made every attempt to look vital and energetic. She would rush downstairs to greet groups passing through the White House. Whenever illness forced her to cancel a public appearance, she laid the blame on food poisoning, concealing how sick she really was.

## A Model of Femininity

High energy has not always marked the history of presidents' wives. Their single most common characteristic has been retirement from the arena of public affairs. Evidence suggests that many of them began as outspoken, adventuresome girls and then ended up quiet shadows of their husbands' fame and success. Stories of Martha Washington's youth suggest she slapped a suitor and led a horse through a parlor, but as First Lady she was quietly polite.

As a young woman, Louisa Adams had traveled by carriage from St.

Although she never learned to drive a car, Florence Harding was an excellent horsewoman—and she rode astride rather than sidesaddle.

When Hillary Rodham Clinton spoke at the United Nations in March 1995, she asked that more attention be given to opening opportunities for women around the world.

Petersburg to Paris with only two young children and two unreliable servants for company; she faced down thieves and talked her way past assassins. But in the White House she is remembered only as an accomplished, charming hostess. Even she failed to credit herself properly, and when she wrote her life story for her children, she titled it "Adventures of a Nobody."

Lucy Hayes gave speeches in college urging equal pay for women, but by the time she became First Lady, she refused to join her female relatives when they asked for her support in getting the vote for women. Caroline Harrison worked for the establishment of the Johns Hopkins Medical School—on the condition it admit women—but she gets into history books mostly because of the china collection she started for the President's House.

Stronger models appeared in the twentieth century, but still within limits. Eleanor Roosevelt carefully disclaimed any voice in Franklin's decisions although she freely admitted to passing along information.

Betty Ford's public announcement that she disagreed with her husband on significant issues has been attributed to her lack of national campaign experience. Barbara Bush's reticence remained the standard tack. She waited until she had moved back to Texas to reveal her views on controversial issues.

Hillary Rodham Clinton appeared to offer a new model, and in the first two years of her White House tenure, she kept a high public profile, chairing the Task Force on Health Care Reform and taking responsibility for having managed the family's finances. But when her forcefulness appeared to create problems for her husband's administration, she drew back. On her trips to Asia in 1995, she made women's issues her priority. When she accompanied the president to Russia in May of that same year, she looked a lot like Pat Nixon—touring museums and schools with the wife of the Russian president and laying wreaths at cemeteries. This avoidance of controversy appeared to many observers as a variation of what reporters had deemed the standard "peeking in the pots" First Lady tour.

The only First Lady born outside the United States, Louisa Adams became adept at American ways by the time she moved into the White House.

As the United States moves into its third century, Americans can look in many directions for female models—movie and television stars, newscasters, business leaders, scientists, athletes, artists, and achievers in many fields. Yet the First Lady's face remains the most recognizable of them all, and her name will continue to appear on *Good Housekeeping*'s list of "Most Admired Women" decades after she has left Washington. People watch what she wears and what she does, how she decorates her home and cuts her hair, when she speaks out and when she keeps quiet. Although she may tailor her image to win approval, she is also setting limits. Unelected and unappointed, she continues to lead.

# After the White House

When Betty Ford left Washington in January 1977, she recognized that only part of her First Lady duties had ended. "It is a job that diminishes," she explained, "but never ends." In the years that followed she continued to operate in the nation's spotlight, battling her own demons of alcoholism and drug dependency, arthritis and breast cancer, while television reporters and gossip columnists scrutinized every move.

Two former First Ladies, Pat Nixon (center) and Betty Ford (right), joined incumbent Barbara Bush (left) at the dedication of the Richard Nixon Library. *(opposite)* Lady Bird Johnson, seated between her daughters, Lynda and Luci, limited her public appearances after leaving Washington. *(above)*

## Duration of Post-Washington Years

Not all First Ladies face life sentences as long as Betty Ford's. Three died in the White House—Letitia Tyler in 1842, Caroline Harrison in 1893, and Ellen Wilson in 1914—and Abigail Fillmore caught cold as she stood listening to the inaugural address of her husband's successor in March 1853, and she died three weeks later.

Most presidents' wives, however, can expect that their post–White House years will exceed the time they spent there. Typically younger than their husbands, the women usually outlive them, partly explaining why former presidents survive an average thirteen years after leaving the job, compared to the First Ladies' twenty-two. Women who are very much younger than their husbands survive them by almost a lifetime.

Since she became First Lady at age twenty-two, it is not surprising that Frances Cleveland holds the record for the number of years she lived after leaving the White House—half a century. Of her twenty-two years as Grover Cleveland's wife, she spent only six years as First Lady. But when she died in 1947, at the age of eighty-three, it was that small, highly publicized fraction of her life that made national headlines.

Frances had led a full life after she left the capital. The Clevelands moved to Princeton, and following Grover's death in 1908, she continued to live there with their four children. In 1913, when she was forty-eight, she remarried, choosing this time a man only two years older than herself and one whose scholarly interests were a far cry from the hurly-burly of politics. Thomas Jex Preston had been a successful businessman before retiring at forty, earning baccalaureate and doctoral degrees in classical archaeology and settling in Princeton. When she married him, Frances became the first (and for more than half a century the only) widow of a president to remarry.

Julia Tyler, the only other young bride of a sitting president—the widowed John Tyler, who was three decades her senior—lived less than one year in the White House. Of the forty-four years she survived after

Frances Cleveland (seated center) poses with her four surviving children and husband in Princeton. Both boys were born after the Clevelands left the White House.

Sarah Polk (seated) lived forty-two years after finishing her single term as First Lady.

leaving Washington, she spent twenty-seven of them as a widow. Rather than remarrying, Julia devoted most of her energy to perpetuating John Tyler's memory—no easy task.

Never a popular man, he was the first to reach the presidency through the back door. In 1840, the Whigs nominated him for vice president without giving the subject much thought. No president had ever died in office, but unfortunately for the Whigs, the sixty-eight-year-old Harrison survived his inauguration by only one month and John Tyler was elevated to the job of chief executive. Virtually a stranger to many Whigs, he did little to please them, thus earning the titles "president without a party" and "Accidental President." He had no chance of winning a second term.

Unceremoniously retired from the capital, the Tylers returned to their 1,600-acre Virginia plantation, Sherwood Forest, where their final years were marked by a combination of personal pleasure and political pain. They remained devoted to each other, and the former president boasted that he still felt like a honeymooner fourteen years after marrying. Julia gave birth to seven children, the last born in 1860 when John was seventy years old. But the national debate over slavery and its expansion into the western territories embroiled the Tylers and complicated their lives.

John stoutly defended the southern point of view as the nation pulled apart, and in 1861 he accepted a seat in the Confederate government. New York–born Julia had already embraced her husband's pro-slavery views, and she wrote caustic letters to her northern relatives and friends, including one published in the *New York Herald,* arguing that the evils of slavery had been exaggerated in the press and in books such as *Uncle Tom's Cabin.*

After John died and the war ended, Julia's public support for the Confederacy tainted her reputation among Unionists, and she paid the price when Congress balked at adding her to the pension list for former

First Ladies. "Surely the wife of a President who served his country so arduously . . . deserves your consideration," she pleaded with legislators. In 1882, they finally relented, giving her the same compensation as Mary Lincoln, Lucretia Garfield, and Sarah Polk. Julia collected $5,000 annually until her death seven years later.

Sarah Polk, another southerner, played her cards better. Her husband died relatively young, three months after his term ended, and she was left to make business decisions on her own for forty years. Only forty-four when she left Washington, Sarah Polk never remarried, although rumors linked her to the bachelor James Buchanan. Her popularity stood so high that she could have boosted his, and pundits suggested that Buchanan might find marriage to Sarah an easy way to "polka" his way into the White House. But he managed to get elected in 1856 without marrying anyone. Just before the Civil War started, Sarah sold her Louisiana plantation and the slaves who worked it, thus cashing in before emancipation. During the fighting, she remained on neutral territory in Tennessee and entertained guests from both sides.

## Grandmothering and Gardening

The long widowhood of Sarah Polk and other former presidents' wives gave them time to do many things. Some traveled, but most devoted themselves to their families and nonpolitical interests. Occasionally invited back to the White House for a dinner or ceremony, they were treated as relics of an earlier time, no longer connected as they once were to movers and doers. Barbara Bush often said that she hoped George would get out of politics while she still had the vigor to garden, and when they returned to Texas in 1993 and began building a new home, she pronounced life "outside the White House just great." Her relief echoed that of many of her predecessors.

Abigail Adams lived seventeen years after vacating the White House, and although politics continued to interest her, she gradually turned

Pat Nixon, who sometimes complained about too much official traveling when her daughters were young, had more time for her grandchildren.

more of her declining energy to her children and their families. Fifty-six years old when John's single term ended, she knew that many people found her out of touch with the times. She had heard herself compared to the woman in a popular ballad about a devoted, elderly couple, "Darby and Joan:" "Sore-eyed Joan tottered about." Abigail had other disappointments. Her only daughter died of breast cancer in 1813 after a troubled marriage to a shiftless husband, and the two Adams sons were busy with their own careers and families.

Had it not been for the reconciliation with her old friend Thomas Jefferson, Abigail might have lost more of her will to live. Years earlier, when the independence movement brought them together, the Adamses became friendly with the tall Virginian, and in 1787, when Jefferson sent for his nine-year-old daughter to join him in Paris, it was Abigail who accompanied her on the Atlantic crossing. A few years later, political differences pushed the two families apart. Abigail blamed Jefferson for heading up the opposition that criticized her husband's leadership and ousted him from office after only one term. Jeffersonian Republicans launched such strong attacks on her family that Abigail broke off all communication with Jefferson, but she could not quite bring herself to renounce the friendship permanently. To her son, she confessed, "There is a little corner of my heart where he once sat as a friend."

In 1804, when word reached her of the death of President Jefferson's daughter at the age of twenty-five, Abigail's grief overwhelmed her pique and she wrote her old friend, "Reasons of various kinds withheld my pen, until the powerful feelings of my heart have burst through the restraint." Jefferson replied, expressing sorrow that "circumstances should have arisen which have seemed to draw a line of separation between us."

The correspondence continued until Abigail's death in 1818—she had signed her last letter to him, "Your old and steady Friend." It remained for John Adams to reply to Jefferson's condolence letter, and, Abigail having brought them together again, the two men continued to exchange news until their deaths, which occurred remarkably on the same day: July 4, 1826, the fiftieth anniversary of the Declaration of Independence. At age ninety-one, John Adams's final words underlined the importance of the friendship. "Thomas Jefferson still survives," he said, not knowing that the Virginian had died three hours earlier.

Dolley Madison never engaged in the heated political debates that Abigail Adams enjoyed, but she was not ignorant of the ideas behind them. After she left the White House, she thrived on a social schedule almost as busy as the one that had made her so popular there. After James Madison died in 1836, she moved back to Washington and reaped the accolades of a grateful nation. Congress voted her the franking privilege and the rarest of tributes—a seat of honor in the visitors' gallery of the

In the seventeen years that Abigail Adams lived after her First Ladyship ended, she had time to renew old friendships.

Of Lady Bird Johnson's seven grandchildren, only two were born while she lived in the White House.

House of Representatives. Presidents and other powerful Washingtonians included her Lafayette Square house on their list of required visits.

Dolley's final years were marred, however, by financial difficulties not entirely her fault. Her one son (from her first marriage) mismanaged her property and squandered her money. When Congress took pity on her and purchased James Madison's papers, the son managed to get his hands on that money as well. Dolley was reduced to traveling to New York and asking for a loan to see her through, until Congress negotiated to buy a second set of papers just before her death.

Louisa Adams's luck was not much better. Like so many nineteenth-century First Ladies, Louisa outlived most of her children. Her only daughter died in infancy. Of Louisa's three sons, the oldest died at sea one month after his parents left the White House and another son died five years later. Only the youngest, Charles Francis, survived at the time of his mother's death in 1852 and could take comfort in Congress's honors: in her memory, the House of Representatives adjourned deliberations to attend her funeral.

Although Louisa Adams's husband served in Congress after completing his White House term, most presidents and their wives preferred retirements that steered clear of politics. Goodwill missions and diplomacy interested the men and utilized their experience, leaving their wives the option of a lower public profile. Lady Bird Johnson, one of the most active and effective of all political wives, was glad for the change. "Politics was Lyndon's life, not mine," she said, "and thirty-seven years were enough." Although she occasionally went to bat for her son-in-law, Senator Charles Robb of Virginia, she refused to speak out in most political contests. Her former chief of staff, Liz Carpenter, admitted that—except for family—wildflowers were her chief interest.

## Making New Lives

The National Wildflower Research Center that Lady Bird founded in Austin, Texas, may eventually stand as her greatest legacy. Established in 1982, more than a decade after the Johnsons left the White House and well after Lyndon's death in 1973, the privately funded center illustrates how a determined First Lady can make a new life for herself after her husband's term ends. With its strong emphasis on working with the environment rather than against it, the center encourages landscaping with native wildflowers rather than high-maintenance imported varieties and manicured lawns. Her national prominence surely assisted Lady Bird Johnson in raising funds, and it is difficult to argue that she could have made the same mark if her husband had not presided over the Oval Office.

Lou Hoover resented voters' rejection of her husband for a second term in 1932, but her many interests (including photography) made for a busy retirement.

Although John Kennedy had not been her first choice for president, Eleanor Roosevelt worked for the Democratic ticket in 1960.

Indeed, the job of First Lady has provided a springboard for several women to fashion successful careers on their own after their husbands' terms ended. Eleanor Roosevelt is perhaps the most remarkable example of how one woman continues to grow at an age when most women contentedly relax. Her biographer, Joseph Lash, devoted one entire volume to chronicling the world travels, writings, and speeches of this extraordinary woman during the seventeen years she survived Franklin.

Eleanor's writing took various forms. After publishing self-help articles in the 1920s, she began a syndicated column, "My Day," in 1936 and continued it until about a month before her death. Books, starting with *It's Up to the Women* in 1933, appeared with such frequency that the list becomes long. Some, such as *India and the Awakening East,* aimed to inspire, while others, such as *Eleanor Roosevelt's Christmas Book,* had more limited objectives.

Politics still claimed part of her time, and one historian called her the "most effective woman in American politics" in the decade after she left the White House. President Truman nominated her to serve as a U.S. delegate to the United Nations, where she helped shape the Universal Declaration of Human Rights. Respect for her grew so great that even old political enemies were converted to admirers. Senator Arthur Vandenberg, who had often opposed her, volunteered to "take back everything I've ever said about her, and believe me it's been plenty." She was widely acclaimed as First Lady of the World.

Grace Coolidge never achieved Eleanor's prominence, but in her own way, she shaped a new life for herself as a widow. After leaving the White House, the Coolidges returned to live in Northampton, Massachusetts, where Grace did her own errands and regained the privacy that had eluded her in Washington. She was even occasionally mistaken for a salesclerk in the local department store.

After Calvin's death in 1933, Grace broadened her list of activities, touring Europe and becoming president of the Clarke school, where she had trained. More willing to give her opinions now than in the White House, Grace told reporters she had not liked *Gone With the Wind* because "the heroine was such a fool." An avid baseball fan, she attended so many games that at the 1951 World Series she was recognized as "First Lady of Baseball."

Although she gave much of her time to her family and the community, Grace Coolidge put a premium on independence. When she built a new house, an unconventional structure with all the living quarters on the second floor, she insisted on tinted bathroom fixtures although the only fixtures that met local building codes came in institutional white. During World War II, she lent her house to the commanding officer of the WAVES (the navy's women's auxiliary corps) and tugged her groceries home in a two-wheeled cart to save gasoline. Her

Grace Coolidge posed with some of the military personnel who used her home during World War II.

serenity indicated that she did not mind managing on her own. Friends recalled an old story about her: As First Lady, she had been enjoying herself at a party when one of the other guests said, "I'm sorry your husband isn't here." "Oh," Grace said, "if he were, I wouldn't be."

Betty Ford also forged a new life after the White House by turning her personal problems to the benefit of others. Her difficulties with alcohol and painkillers surfaced after she retired to California, although she later admitted that she had developed a dependence years earlier, when she began suffering from a pinched nerve and arthritis. Only after a confrontation with her family in 1978 did she enter a hospital and admit to being an alcoholic. After she successfully completed therapy, she lent her name to centers where others could go for help, and by the 1990s, when Americans talked of "going to Betty Ford," they meant the treatment center, not the woman.

The former First Lady's candor about her own health problems made her a popular figure, and in 1987, with her cooperation, ABC/TV produced a two-hour movie, *The Betty Ford Story.* It coincided with the publication of her second book, *Betty—A Glad Awakening,* in which she detailed more fully than before her alcoholism and recovery. Two decades after leaving Washington, her schedule looked a lot like that of a busy executive—lobbying for legislation, traveling across the country to raise funds for the Betty Ford Center, and working with staff to make major decisions.

Jacqueline Kennedy had little use for such candor and self-revelation, and she worked hard to keep her post–White House years as private as possible. Her life had neatly divided into halves by the time she died in 1994—she lived thirty-one years before becoming First Lady and thirty-one years afterward.

Carving out a new life for herself after she left Washington, she married Greek shipping magnate Aristotle Onassis in 1968, but following his death six years later, she established firmer roots in New York. Taking a

job first at Viking Press, then moving on to Doubleday & Co., where her former social secretary also worked, she edited about ten books a year, many of them on the arts. Although her liaison with Belgian-born Maurice Templesman lasted longer than either of her marriages. Jacqueline maintained a long list of her own interests, including the American Ballet Theatre (where she encouraged the ailing dancer Rudolph Nureyev to try conducting)  and preservation of landmark buildings.

**Jacqueline Kennedy Onassis took time away from editing to sit with granddaughter Rose in New York's Central Park.**

## Some Public Compensations

Americans are reluctant to forget a popular First Lady, and some of the recognition comes from Congress. Beginning with Martha Washington, presidents' widows have been permitted free use of the mails, providing they asked for the right to frank their letters by signing their names on the envelope. Most applied for the frank (although Abigail Adams and Eliza Johnson did not, and Ida McKinley generally paid postage in order to conserve her energy). Nineteenth-century women tended to use their own names or initials (D. P. Madison, L. C. Adams, and Lucretia Garfield) rather than their husbands' names (Mrs. Lyndon Johnson). Although she had the right to sign, Edith Wilson had a facsimile made to speed up the process.

Frances Cleveland's remarriage in 1913 presented a problem and raised the question of exactly how she had earned the frank she had been using since 1909. If she had received the privilege because of her own six years as First Lady, then her remarriage should have no effect; but if she had received it on the strength of her late husband's tenure as chief executive, remarriage might terminate it. The question was settled when, without any apparent public objection, Frances merely added her new husband's name and, signing herself "Frances Cleveland Preston," continued sending her mail for free until her death in 1947.

The idea of pensions for presidents' widows developed more slowly, beginning in 1841 when Anna Harrison's husband died in office. Because he had served little of his term and his wife was less than wealthy, Congress voted to pay her a sum equivalent to the president's salary for one year. Had Congress given her a pension for life, Anna Harrison would have fared better, because she survived another twenty-three years, outliving all but one of her children and dying at age eighty-eight.

The circumstances of Abraham Lincoln's death in 1865 differed so much from William Henry Harrison's that Mary Lincoln thought she

Edith Roosevelt spoke at a rally for Herbert Hoover in 1932—when the opponent was Franklin D. Roosevelt, husband of Edith's niece, Eleanor. *(above)* Mary Lincoln's penchant for excessive spending continued to cause her difficulties after her husband's death. *(opposite)*

deserved a more generous compensation. Her husband's murder was the first of a president, and Mary suffered the trauma of witnessing it. In the manner of many martyrs, she placed a high monetary value on her suffering, and for the remainder of her life she lobbied for a liberal settlement.

Insecure about money all her life, Mary Lincoln became obsessed by the subject in her widowhood. Her husband's will left $35,000 to her and to each of their surviving sons—a sum larger than the chief executive's annual salary at the time—so she was hardly poor, but, fearing poverty, she decided to auction off her old clothing. Although she used an assumed name in her advertisements and worked out of a hotel room in New York City, news leaked that the president's widow was behaving like a street vendor. To escape criticism and other embarrassments, she sailed for Europe, where she thought she could live more cheaply. But she continued to read the newspapers, and when Congress voted her a pension of $3,000 in 1870, she returned to Illinois.

If she had hoped that her final years would be tranquil, Mary Lincoln was surely disappointed. Stories about her husband's youthful infatuation with Ann Rutledge continued to embarrass her, although there was little basis for them in fact. Tad Lincoln, Mary's youngest, died in 1871, and her one surviving son, Robert, remained cold and distant. The strained relationship between mother and son deteriorated even further when he asked for a court decision on her sanity in 1875. Alarmed by reports that she dabbled in spiritualism and carried her life savings sewed into her skirt, Robert had her confined to a mental institution outside Chicago.

The records of the private hospital reveal a moody woman who changed her mind often but was hardly insane: she would order a dish for breakfast and then decline to eat it, request a carriage and refuse to budge. She shrewdly plotted her release. Relying on powerful people she had once known, she summoned journalists and legislators to visit her, and one of the callers, Myra Bradwell, the first woman lawyer in Illinois, pronounced her "no more insane than I am." A reporter concluded that Mary showed "not a sign of weakness of mind."

Released from the hospital, Mary Lincoln went to live in France, but after a bad fall and partial paralysis, she returned to her sister's home in Illinois, where she died in 1882. The end could not have come too soon, according to one of Mary's shipmates on the Atlantic crossing: the famous actress Sarah Bernhardt later described how she had befriended the president's widow and saved her from a bad fall down a flight of stairs. Bernhardt realized, she later admitted, that she had done the one thing for Mary Lincoln that she should not have done—saved her life.

Just a few months before Mary Lincoln's death, Congress increased the pensions for presidents' widows to $5,000 but retained the right to approve each applicant individually. Some women hesitated to apply, and Edith Roosevelt explained that she acted reluctantly. Although in comfortable circumstances herself, she was persuaded by the argument that if she did not apply, other women who were truly in need would be embarrassed to reveal their circumstances.

The record shows considerable variation. Julia Grant collected a pension within months of Ulysses's death but Helen Taft waited seven years to present her case. Mary Harrison (who married the widowed Benjamin Harrison after he left the White House and thus never served as First Lady) did not begin collecting until 1938, thirty-seven years after her husband's death, although she had been using the franking privilege for three decades. Frances Cleveland did not receive a pension until 1940, long after she had remarried.

Some compensation may be seen as substituting for a salary never paid since Congress has occasionally talked of remunerating the president's wife. In 1946, Republican Congressman James G. Fulton of Pennsylvania proposed an annual salary of $10,000, saying the nation provided for widows but did little for the "wives who are in there work-

One of the last photographs of Lucy Hayes showed her at a favorite pastime—feeding pigeons.

Although she left the White House in 1921, Edith Galt Wilson (seated on right) remained a celebrity in Washington for forty more years.

ing on their job every day." Incumbent Bess Truman made no comment on the subject, and the proposal was quickly dropped as being unauthorized by law. Betty Ford once suggested that First Ladies deserve a salary but later insisted she had spoken in jest. She well understood that Americans expect a "two-fer" president—one elected and drawing a salary and the other an unpaid spouse who comes along.

## The Respect and Curiosity of a Nation

Some women have reaped substantial benefits, intangible as well as monetary, from short tenures in the White House. Whether in social status or perquisites not easily given a price tag, the compensations mount up. Edith Galt Wilson's eight-year marriage to Woodrow propelled her to the peak of Washington society and launched her celebrity status that lasted through the forty years she lived as his widow. Presidents sought her company, journalists curried her favor, and she remained a public personage until her death.

Lucretia Garfield used a briefer tenure as First Lady to even greater advantage. Her husband's death in 1881 ended her White House residency after less than six months, but not before the American public had developed enormous respect for her dignity and strength. James Garfield's assassin, a deranged office seeker, had shot him in the Washington train station in July, but the president lingered until late September, suffering through a sweltering summer before he succumbed. As Americans followed newspaper accounts of his condition week after week, they became familiar with his children and developed a special respect for the First Lady who kept vigil at his bedside.

At his death, contributions poured into the White House from across the nation, and more than $360,000 was raised for the Garfield family. Lucretia took her children back to their home in Ohio and lived the remaining thirty-six years of her life as a national saint. She traveled across the country in a special railway car, penned her notes on black bordered paper, and received the homage of a grateful nation.

Jacqueline Kennedy also earned the permanent respect of her country for the way she handled herself in the aftermath of assassination. Only thirty-four years old when John Kennedy was murdered, she maintained a composure during the days and weeks that followed that amazed many of her critics and provided her with an almost invulnerable protective shield of public affection. During a later dispute with

The Garfield children gained the nation's sympathy after their father's assassination in 1881.

Jacqueline Kennedy's dignity at her husband's funeral moved millions of Americans.

writer William Manchester, she warned him that unless she ran off with a movie star, Americans would side with her on any controversial issue, including her disagreement with him.

Jackie's composure on the weekend of the assassination had been remarkable. Only ninety-nine minutes after seeing her husband killed as he sat beside her, she stood alongside Lyndon B. Johnson as he was sworn in as the thirty-sixth president of the United States. Then she flew back to Washington on *Air Force One* and directed arrangements for a funeral that equaled the drama of Abraham Lincoln's funeral nearly a century earlier.

After lying in state in the Capitol rotunda, the coffin of the slain president was moved on a horse-drawn caisson followed by a riderless horse, the symbol of a fallen leader. The president's young widow and two brothers walked behind, a stark reminder of the nation's loss. After the funeral she stood to receive world leaders, and the very next day, she showed her successor around the executive mansion. Before moving out, she sent the bloodstained pink suit she had been wearing in Dallas to be stored, together with the matching pillbox hat, shoes, and handbag, at the National Archives.

A short residence in Georgetown failed to provide the privacy the young widow wanted for her children and herself, and during the summer of 1964, she purchased a fifteen-room cooperative apartment on New York's Fifth Avenue. But even the metropolis could not shield her from the world's enormous curiosity. Photographers and reporters trailed along when she jogged, escorted her children to school, or lunched with her sister. Friends reported that she found her greatest pleasure in watching the progress of Caroline and John, and she frequently said that raising them was "the best thing I have ever done."

## Writing about Their Lives

Jacqueline Kennedy never wrote a full account of her own life or encouraged others to do it for her, but by the time she died Americans had come to expect that former First Ladies would do at least one book. Although many appear prompted by a sense of history and their own place in it, the first to do so, Julia Grant, was motivated partly by her need for money. The heirs of some of her predecessors had spliced together memoirs out of their letters, but Julia was the first president's wife to write in the hopes of sales. Her husband's book, completed just before he died in 1885, eventually earned nearly half a million dollars in

Lady Bird Johnson's *White House Diary* includes only part of the hundreds of hours of tapes that she made as First Lady.

royalties, and although she could not match his success, she could help set the record straight. Unfortunately, her manuscript failed to find a publisher until 1975, long after she and all her children were dead.

In writing about her own life, Julia used less than a tenth of the book to talk about the White House years, and most of that dealt with her social accomplishments and her husband's innocence in a major scandal. Ulysses's role in the 1874 gold market debacle had never been clarified during his lifetime, although there were many versions. When financiers Jim Fisk and Jay Gould attempted to corner the gold market and enrich themselves by several million dollars, they apparently enlisted the help of President Grant's brother-in-law, believing—incorrectly, as it turned out—that they had the president's concurrence as well. Julia adamantly declared Ulysses's hands clean. He had warned his sister, through Julia herself, to have nothing to do with Fisk and his schemes because "come what may," Ulysses meant to do right by the country and uphold his oath of office.

If Julia's immediate successors knew of her book, they chose not to imitate her. Lucy Hayes disliked writing and often prevailed on her husband to pen her letters for her. Other First Ladies lacked either the self-confidence or the inclination to reveal much about themselves. But Helen Taft, never one to hold back, may have been bitten by the same bug that stung Julia Grant. In 1914, less than two years after leaving the White House, she became the first First Lady to publish her autobiography during her lifetime. Helen used more than half of the 395 pages to describe the four years she and her family lived in the Philippines and only a fraction as much for the major reason for the book's sales—her four years in the White House.

Edith Galt Wilson waited longer. Two decades after Americans had debated her role as "Assistant President," she published her version of what really happened. Some of the stories in her autobiography contradicted others that she had previously told, and readers were unsure which account was accurate (if either), but Edith remained firm in her declaration that her power during the president's illness had been exaggerated. "I studied every paper," she wrote, "but I myself never made a single decision regarding the disposition of public affairs."

Lady Bird Johnson must have had publication in mind as she faithfully recorded her White House experiences in a tiny tape recorder. Her reasons, she wrote, were two. First, she realized shortly after the assassination that "I stood in a unique position. . . . Nobody else would live through the next months in quite the way that I would and see the events unroll from this vantage point." The second involved discipline: "I wanted to see if I could keep up this arduous task." In hotel rooms, her bedroom at the LBJ ranch, and at her desk overlooking the Rose Garden, she spoke for hundreds of hours. *A White House Diary,* published in 1970, is culled from those tapes, giving her insights into the five years and two months she served as First Lady.

An enormously private Pat Nixon showed no interest in following suit. She had worked hard at the job, as the appointment books of her secretaries prove, and she had gamely gone along on foreign junkets ever since Dwight Eisenhower, recognizing her enormous popularity, advised then Vice President Richard Nixon to "take Pat along." But she showed no interest in telling her side of the story. "In this job, you know a lot," she once said, "but you have to keep quiet." She applied the same rules to her post–White House years as to the time in Washington.

Her daughter, Julie Nixon Eisenhower, waited for more than a decade after her father's resignation and then wrote *Pat Nixon: The Untold Story.* Only the last thirty pages discuss the post–White House years, although that period may have been most pleasurable. Pat dealt with her husband's major illnesses and her own, but she finally had time of her own. "Her chosen world was creating a home," Julie wrote, and she found joy in concocting unusual flower arrangements and in reading, averaging five books a week. The woman who left the South Lawn

Pat Nixon, who had long disliked political life, got her chance to leave Washington and return to California in 1974.

When Bess Truman (second from left) returned for a visit to the Kennedy White House, staff recalled what a popular First Lady she had been with them. *(above)* Rosalynn Carter (left) and Betty Ford continued to play strong public roles after leaving the White House. *(opposite)*

of the White House, saying that she was "sick" of red carpets, finally got away from them.

Another retiring but popular First Lady, Bess Truman, also left it for her daughter to tell her side of the story, but Margaret Truman Daniel waited until after her mother's death in 1982 to publish *Bess W. Truman*. The timing may have resulted partly from Bess's feelings about her father's death, which haunted her the rest of her life. Journalists respected her feelings and refused to write about it while she lived. Finally, after Bess's death, Margaret told the story in as much detail as she could reconstruct.

Rosalynn Carter had no intention of leaving to her daughter the task of writing her story. Two years after she returned to Georgia, she

National Press Club

Mrs. Betty Fo

After finishing eight years as First Lady, Nancy Reagan's main concern was looking after her husband's health and well-being.

published *First Lady from Plains.* Reviewers praised it as an excellent account of the Carter presidency, and critics wrote that some sections were far more illuminating than those by Jimmy and his associates.

Not content to retire from the public arena in 1981, Rosalynn continued to keep a full schedule. Teaming up with her husband, she wrote books on aging and helped on projects of Habitat for Humanity, a volunteer effort to provide low-cost housing for poor families. When Jimmy undertook independent diplomatic ventures in the 1990s, she was actively involved. It was her advice, he later said, that persuaded him to talk with the entire family of Haiti's acting dictator and help negotiate the general's departure. Although many people denigrated the Carter peace mission to the Caribbean, he was invited to troubled Bosnia a few weeks later. This time Rosalynn went along. She was, the *New York Times*

noted, one of only three assistants who accompanied Jimmy.

Nancy Reagan had played such a prominent part in her husband's presidency that no one imagined she would slide into obscurity when it ended. Working with William Novak, who had helped turn Lee Iococca's story into a best-seller, she published *My Turn* in 1989. Jacket copy quoted her as saying she had always found "a certain dignity in silence" but that she had decided "for the historical record" to tell her side of the story. Although she continued to head the Nancy Reagan Foundation, which provided millions of dollars of grants to drug prevention and education programs, most of her energy went, as it had throughout her marriage, to helping her husband. She spent most of her time with him; she was beside him when he underwent brain surgery at Mayo Clinic in 1989 and again when the announcement came in late

Barbara Bush often said she hoped her husband would leave politics while she still had the vigor to garden and enjoy her grandchildren.

1994 that he suffered from Alzheimer's disease.

Barbara Bush had always played her public role very differently from Nancy Reagan, and her autobiography underscores the contrast. Called simply *Barbara Bush,* the 532-page memoir shows every evidence of being written by her—as she insisted it was—on her own laptop computer. Her husband, slower to get his story on paper, had not completed his book when hers came out in 1994 and immediately claimed a place on the best-seller lists. Readers looking for revelations were disappointed. Most of the stories had been reported before, but the book underlined her ebullient optimism. "No man, woman, or child ever had a better life," she said in the preface, noting that in recounting it, she had used "wonderful" so many times that her editor rationed her to one per page. Some critics pronounced the restriction too lenient—they would have liked fewer superlatives and more insight—but Barbara, always confidently herself, told her story her way.

## Choice of Burial Place

One subject that presidents' wives avoided in their books involved burial plans, although curious Americans watched closely when decisions were made. Interest was especially keen when either the chief executive or his wife had been married more than once, and speculation was rife when Jacqueline Kennedy Onassis died in 1994. She chose interment at Arlington National Cemetery near the graves of John F. Kennedy and their two children who had died in infancy, rather than beside her more recent spouse, Aristotle Onassis.

The former First Lady was merely following tradition. Her predecessors had also chosen burial beside the husbands who took them to the White House—even if they'd had other husbands before or after the president. Not all had a voice in the matter. Ellen Wilson was buried in a family plot in Georgia when she died in 1914, but by the time Woodrow Wilson died in 1924, his second wife was calling the shots.

Although Edith Galt Wilson had lived with Woodrow only eight years (far less than the twenty-nine he and Ellen spent together), she chose interment for him—and herself later—at the National Cathedral in the District of Columbia, making the Wilsons the only presidential couple to be buried in the capital itself.

Edith Wilson apparently never considered burial beside her first husband, Norman Galt, father of her only child, but in this choice she was not unique. Martha Washington, Dolley Madison, and Florence Harding made similar decisions. They were interred by their second husbands, the presidents, rather than by men they first married and whose children they bore.

The death of Caroline Harrison's husband in 1901, nine years after she had died, gave the public a glimpse into conflict in a president's family. Caroline had lived almost forty years as Benjamin Harrison's wife

Eleanor Roosevelt told reporters, "The story is over," when her husband died, but then she went on to make an important life for herself.

At Richard Nixon's funeral, four former First Ladies and one incumbent joined their husbands.

(including nearly four as First Lady), and she probably would have expected that he would eventually be buried beside her. But he had remarried, choosing this time a much younger woman (who happened to be Caroline's niece) who outlived him by many years. The president's adult children, who never approved the remarriage and refused to be reconciled with their father afterward, saw to it that their mother got the place of honor at his side in the cemetery. Second wife Mary Scott Dimmick Harrison, who died in 1948, had to settle for a plot a short distance away.

Eleanor Roosevelt evidently never questioned that she would be buried at Hyde Park. The Roosevelts typically chose family cemeteries, and her uncle Theodore and aunt Edith had been interred near their Long Island home. Perhaps Eleanor was too busy with a full schedule to give the subject much thought. She had not really predicted the independence she developed in widowhood, and when she returned to New York City in 1945, she had told reporters, "The story is over." But of course it was not. Like Betty Ford and others, Eleanor Roosevelt soon learned that the end of a president's term, or even his death, no more relieves his wife of the spotlight of public attention than it delivers him into obscurity. When Eleanor died in 1962, her family chose for her tombstone only her name and the dates of her birth and death. The rest would be written by others.

Harry Truman did not want to leave such things to chance or to others. Before he died in 1972, he settled on Bess's epitaph: "First Lady, the United States of America / April 12, 1945–January 20, 1953." He had singled out the time that had been central to her life—and a responsibility ended only by her death.

....................................................................

Whether their tenures lasted a few months or several years, most presidents' wives enjoyed White House living. True, there were difficulties, but the advantages usually outweighed them, and more than one woman expressed her gratitude. Lady Bird Johnson voiced "amazement" that it happened to her; Barbara Bush recalled "four extraordinary years"; Nancy Reagan admitted that she "would not trade those experiences for anything"; Hillary Rodham Clinton spoke of the chance "to make a difference." Aware of what they share, America's First Ladies support each other across party and generation lines—while a curious nation watches.

# Appendix

## ADAMS, Abigail Smith

Born on November 22, 1744, in Weymouth, Massachusetts, she died a few miles away in Quincy, Massachusetts, on October 28, 1818. Married to John Adams (1735–1826) in 1764, she gave birth to five children, four of whom reached adulthood. Her husband served two terms as vice president (1789–1797) and one as president (1797–1801). She died before her son became president in 1825.

## ADAMS, Louisa Catherine Johnson

Born on February 12, 1775, in London, she died on May 14, 1852, in Washington. D.C. Married to John Quincy Adams in 1797, she gave birth to three sons who survived infancy and to at least two other children who did not, including a daughter who was born and died in Russia. John Quincy Adams's single term as president lasted from 1825 to 1829.

## ARTHUR, Ellen Lewis Herndon

Born on August 30, 1837, in Culpepper, Virginia, she died in New York City on January 12, 1880, shortly before her husband was nominated for vice president. She married Chester Arthur on October 25, 1859, and they had three children, two of whom survived childhood. Her husband was inaugurated president following the death of James Garfield in September, 1881, and he served the remainder of that term.

## BUSH, Barbara Pierce

Born on June 8, 1925, in New York City, she married George Bush in 1945. They had four children who reached adulthood and one daughter who died in childhood. George Bush was president for one term—from January 1989 to January 1993.

## CARTER, Rosalynn Smith

Born near Plains, Georgia, on August 18, 1927, she married Jimmy Carter in 1946. They had four children. Her husband's presidency lasted one term—from January 1977 until January 1981.

Barbara Bush with an AIDS baby *(above)* and Rosalyn Carter at a refugee camp *(opposite)* both worked to improve chidren's lives.

Hillary Rodham Clinton was the first president's wife born after World War II.

### CLEVELAND, Frances Folsom

Born on July 21, 1864, in Buffalo, New York, she died on October 29, 1947, in Baltimore, Maryland. Married in the White House to Grover Cleveland on June 2, 1886, she served as First Lady for the remainder of his term. He was not reelected in 1888 but returned to the White House in 1893 for a second term, so she lived nearly six years there. Their first daughter (born in 1891) died at age twelve, but four other children reached adulthood. Grover Cleveland died in 1908, and his widow married Thomas Jex Preston in 1913.

### CLINTON, Hillary Rodham

Born on October 26, 1947, she married Bill Clinton in 1975 and they had one daughter. The Clinton administration began on January 20, 1993.

### COOLIDGE, Grace Goodhue

Born on January 3, 1879, in Burlington, Vermont, she died on July 8, 1957, in Northampton, Massachusetts. Married to Calvin Coolidge in 1905, she had two sons, one of whom died in Washington during the Coolidge presidency. Calvin Coolidge became president on the death of Warren Harding in August 1923 and completed that term, then served one entire term of his own, from 1925 to 1929.

### EISENHOWER, Mamie Doud

Born on November 14, 1896, in Boone, Iowa, she died on November 1, 1979, in Washington, D.C. From her marriage to Dwight D. Eisenhower in 1916 were born two sons, one of whom survived to adulthood. Her husband's two administrations lasted from January 1953 until January 1961.

## FILLMORE, Abigail Powers

Born on March 17, 1798, in Stillwater, New York, she died on March 30, 1853, in Washington, D.C. Married to Millard Fillmore on February 5, 1826, she had two children. Her husband became president in July 1850 (when Zachary Taylor suddenly died), and he served the remainder of that term, which ended March 4, 1853.

## FORD, Elizabeth ("Betty") Bloomer Warren

Born on April 18, 1918, in Chicago, she married William Warren, a man from her hometown of Grand Rapids. They were divorced after five years; there were no children. She married Gerald Ford in 1948, and they had four children. Her tenure as First Lady lasted from August 9, 1974 (when Gerald Ford became president at the resignation of Richard Nixon), until January 1977.

## GARFIELD, Lucretia Rudolph

Born on April 19, 1832, in Garretsville, Ohio, she died on March 14, 1918, in South Pasadena, California. After her marriage to James Garfield in 1858, she gave birth to seven children, of whom five survived childhood. Her husband served only briefly as president. Inaugurated in March 1881, he was shot in July and incapacitated until his death on September 19.

## GRANT, Julia Dent

Born January 26, 1826, near St. Louis, Missouri, she died on December 14, 1902, in Washington, D.C. Married to Ulysses Grant on August 22, 1848, she had four children. Her husband's presidency lasted two terms, from March 1869 to March 1877.

## HARDING, Florence Kling DeWolfe

Born on August 15, 1860, in Marion, Ohio, she died there on November 21, 1924. Married to Henry A. DeWolfe in 1880, she had one son. Details of her divorce from DeWolfe are not clear; he died in 1894. In 1891 she married Warren G. Harding. They had no children. Her husband's presidency, begun in March 1921, ended with his death on August 2, 1923.

## HARRISON, Anna Symmes

Born on July 25, 1775, in Morristown, New Jersey, she died on February 25, 1864, in North Bend, Ohio. She married William Henry Harrison in 1795 and gave birth to nine children, including one son (John), whose own son (Benjamin) later became president of the United States. Anna Harrison had not left Ohio to go to Washington in 1841 when she learned that her husband had died, so she never served as First Lady.

## HARRISON, Caroline Lavinia Scott

Born on October 10, 1832, in Oxford, Ohio, she died on October 25, 1892, in the White House. Married to Benjamin Harrison in 1853, she had two children. Her husband's single term as president began in March 1889, but she died shortly before it ended four years later. On April 6, 1896, Benjamin Harrison married the widowed niece of his first wife—Mary Scott Lord Dimmick—and they had one daughter.

A serious student, Lucy Webb Hayes became a popular First Lady.

## HAYES, Lucy Ware Webb

Born on August 28, 1831, in Chillicothe, Ohio, she died on June 25, 1889, in Fremont, Ohio. Married to Rutherford Hayes in 1852, she had eight children, of whom five survived infancy. Her husband's single term as president lasted from March 1877 to March 1881.

## HOOVER, Lou Henry

Born on March 29, 1874, in Waterloo, Iowa, she died on January 7, 1944, in New York City. Married to Herbert Hoover in 1899, she had two sons. Her husband's single term as president lasted from 1929 to 1933.

## JACKSON, Rachel Donelson Robards

Born in western Virginia on June 17, 1767, she died on December 22, 1828, at the Jackson plantation near Nashville, Tennessee. Details of her first marriage (to Lewis Robards in 1785) and subsequent divorce are not clear, but she married Andrew Jackson in August 1791. After questions were raised about whether or not her divorce had been final by 1791, Rachel and Andrew Jackson exchanged wedding vows again in 1794. She had no children. Since she died just as her husband was preparing to go to Washington for his inauguration as president, she never served as First Lady.

## JEFFERSON, Martha Wayles Skelton

Born on October 30, 1748, in Charles County, Virginia, she died on September 6, 1782, at Monticello in childbirth. Her first marriage, to Bathurst Skelton in 1766, ended with his death two years later. She married Thomas Jefferson in 1772 and gave birth to six children, only three of whom survived her. One of these died a few years later, leaving only two daughters to reach adulthood. The elder of these, Martha Jefferson Randolph (1772–1836), occasionally served as White House hostess during her father's presidency (1801–1809).

## JOHNSON, Eliza McCardle

Born on October 4, 1810, in Greeneville, Tennessee, she died there on January 15, 1876. Married to Andrew Johnson in 1827, she had five children. Her husband became president when Abraham Lincoln died in April 1865 and served the remainder of the term, which ended in March 1869.

## JOHNSON, Claudia Alta ("Lady Bird") Taylor

Born on December 22, 1912, in Karnack, Texas, she married Lyndon Johnson in 1934. They had two daughters. Lyndon Johnson became president soon after John Kennedy was assassinated in 1963. After completing that term, he served one term of his own, from 1965 to 1969.

## KENNEDY, Jacqueline Bouvier

Born on July 28, 1929, on Long Island, she died on May 19, 1994, in New York City. From her marriage to John F. Kennedy in 1953 were born two children who reached adulthood. First Lady from January 1961 until her husband's assassination in November 1963, she married Aristotle Onassis in 1968.

## LINCOLN, Mary Todd

Born December 13, 1818, in Lexington, Kentucky, she died on July 16, 1882, in Springfield, Illinois. Married to Abraham Lincoln in 1842, she had four sons; one died at age four, one died at twelve, and a third died at eighteen. Her husband's presidency ended with his assassination in April 1865.

## MCKINLEY, Ida Saxton

Born on June 8, 1847, in Canton, Ohio, she died there on May 26, 1907. Married to William McKinley in 1871, she had two daughters, both of whom died in childhood. Her husband served only one complete term as president (1897–1901) but was assassinated in September 5, 1901, soon after beginning a second term.

## MADISON, Dorothea ("Dolley") Payne Todd

Born on May 20, 1768, in Guilford County, North Carolina, she died on July 12, 1849, in Washington. First married to John Todd, Jr., who died in 1793, she was left with one son, not quite two years old. She married James Madison in 1794. They had no children. During her husband's two terms (1809–1817), she served as First Lady, a role she had often played earlier at President Jefferson's White House.

## MONROE, Elizabeth Kortright

Neither the exact date nor the place of her birth is known, but the date is generally given as 1763 and the place—New York City. She died at Oak Hill, the Monroes' home in Loudoun County, Virginia, on September 23, 1830. Married to James Monroe in 1786, she had two daughters who reached adulthood and one son who died in infancy. James Monroe served as president from 1817 to 1825.

Pat Nixon posed with her daughters and their famous dog, "Checkers."

### NIXON, Patricia "Pat" Ryan

Born on March 16, 1912, in Ely, Nevada, she died on June 22, 1993, at Park Ridge, New Jersey. Married to Richard Nixon in 1940, she had two daughters. Her husband's presidency lasted from January 1969 until his resignation on August 9, 1974.

### PIERCE, Jane Means Appleton

Born on March 12, 1806, in Hampton, New Hampshire, she died on December 2, 1863, in Andover, New Hampshire. Married to Franklin Pierce on November 19, 1834, she had three sons, but all of them died before reaching adulthood. Franklin Pierce's single term as president lasted from 1853 to 1857.

### POLK, Sarah Childress

Born in Rutherford County, Tennessee, on September 4, 1803, she died at Nashville, Tennessee, on August 14, 1891. Married to James Polk in 1824, she had no children. Her husband's presidency lasted one term—from 1845 to 1849.

### REAGAN, Nancy Davis

Born Anne Frances Robbins on July 6, 1921, in New York City, she changed her name to Nancy Davis after her mother married Loyal Davis. Married to Ronald Reagan in 1952, Nancy had two children. Her husband's presidency lasted two terms—from January 1981 until January 1989.

### ROOSEVELT, Alice Hathaway Lee

Born on July 29, 1861, in Chestnut Hill, Massachusetts, she died in New York City on February 14, 1884, while her husband served in the New York State Legislature. She had married Theodore Roosevelt on October 27, 1880, and her death occurred shortly after she gave birth to a daughter (who was also named Alice).

## ROOSEVELT, Edith Kermit Carow

Born on August 6, 1861, in Norwich, Connecticut, she died on September 30, 1948, at Sagamore Hill, the family estate near Oyster Bay, Long Island, New York. Married to Theodore Roosevelt in London in 1886, she had five children. Her husband became president in September 1901, following the assassination of William McKinley, and he was elected to a term of his own, from March 1905 to March 1909.

## ROOSEVELT, Anna Eleanor Roosevelt

Born on October 11, 1884, in New York City, she died there on November 7, 1962. Married to Franklin Roosevelt in 1905, she had six children, one of whom died in infancy. Her husband, first inaugurated president in March 1933, served three complete terms and had just begun a fourth when he died in April 1945.

## TAFT, Helen Herron

Born in 1861 in Cincinnati, Ohio, she died on May 22, 1943, in Washington, D.C. Married to William Howard Taft on June 19, 1886, she had three children. Her husband's single term as president lasted from March 1909 until March 1913.

## TAYLOR, Margaret Mackall Smith

Born on September 21, 1788, in Calvert County, Maryland, she died on August 18, 1852, near Pascagoula, Mississippi. Married to Zachary Taylor in 1810, she gave birth to five daughters and one son, but two of the daughters died in childhood. Her husband's presidency lasted from March 1849 until his death in July 1850.

A young mother, Eleanor Roosevelt, is shown with her husband and only daughter, Anna.

## TRUMAN, Elizabeth ("Bess") Wallace

Born on February 13, 1885, in Independence Missouri, she died there on October 18, 1982. Married to Harry S Truman in 1919, she had one daughter. Her husband's presidency began in April 1945 (following the death of Franklin D. Roosevelt) and ended in January 1953.

## TYLER, Julia Gardiner

Born on May 4, 1820, on Gardiners Island, New York, she died on July 10, 1889, in Richmond, Virginia. Married to John Tyler on June 26, 1844, just months before his term ended in March 1845, she served only briefly as First Lady. She had seven children, all born after John Tyler's presidency ended.

## TYLER, Letitia Christian

Born on November 12, 1790, in New Kent County, Virginia, she died on September 10, 1842, at the White House. Married to John Tyler in 1813, she had seven children who survived infancy. In 1839 her oldest son, Robert, married Priscilla Cooper, an actress, and after John Tyler became president in April 1841, Priscilla often served as White House hostess—a role that ended with the president's remarriage in 1844.

## VAN BUREN, Hannah Hoes

Born on March 8, 1783, in Kinderhook, New York, she died February 5, 1819, in Albany, New York, after giving birth to a fourth son. She married Martin Van Buren in 1807 but died well before he became president in 1837.

## WASHINGTON, Martha Dandridge Custis

Born in New Kent County, Virginia, on June 21, 1731, she died at the Mt. Vernon estate (Virginia) on May 22, 1802. In 1749 she married Daniel Parke Custis, who was twenty years her senior, and they had four children: two who died in infancy, John ("Jackie"), and Martha ("Patsy"). Widowed in 1757, she married George Washington (1732–1799) in 1759. They had no children. His presidency lasted two terms, from April 30, 1789, to March 4, 1797.

## WILSON, Edith Bolling Galt

Born on October 15, 1872, in Wytheville, Virginia, she died on December 28, 1961, in Washington, D.C. In 1896 she married Norman Galt, and they had one son who died in infancy. Norman Galt died in 1908. On December 18, 1915, she married Woodrow Wilson, then completing his first term as president. His second term lasted until March 1921.

## WILSON, Ellen Axson

Born on May 15, 1860, in Savannah, Georgia, she died at the White House on August 6, 1914. Following marriage to Woodrow Wilson in 1885, she had three daughters. Her husband was inaugurated president on March 4, 1913, but she died seventeen months later.

# Further Reading

Anthony, Carl Sferrazza. *First Ladies.* 2 vols. New York: William Morrow and Co., 1990–1991.

Caroli, Betty Boyd. *First Ladies.* New York: Oxford University Press, 1987, expanded ed. 1995.

Gould, Lewis L., ed. *American First Ladies: Their Lives and Their Legacy.* New York: Garland, 1996.

Gutin, Myra G. *The President's Partner: The First Lady in the Twentieth Century.* Westport, Connecticut: Greenwood Press, 1989.

Smith, Nancy Kegan, and Ryan, Mary C., eds. *Modern First Ladies: Their Documentary Legacy.* Washington, D.C.: National Archives and Records Administration, 1989.

Truman, Margaret. *First Ladies.* New York: Random House, 1995.

# Photo Credits

*Grateful acknowledgment is made to the sources whose photographs and illustrations appear on the following pages:*

AP/Wide World Photos: 8, 27, 37, 56, 156

Bush Presidential Materials Project: 62, 82, 102, 146, 151, 169, 201, 207, 216

The Carter Center: 199, 206

Jimmy Carter Library: 5 (bottom), 16, 57, 66, 71

Ed Clark, LIFE Magazine © Time, Inc.: 99, 112

Coolidge Collection at Forbes Library: 24, 96, 114, 186, 218

Culver Pictures: 123, 129

Suzanne de Chillo/NYT Pictures: 116

Dwight D. Eisenhower Library: xiv, 17, 51, 147, 157

Gerald R. Ford Library: 11, 63, 74, 124, 153, 168, 219

Harding Home; Ohio Historical Society: 101, 171

Rutherford B. Hayes Presidential Center: 36, 89, 120, 140,191

The Hermitage: Home of President Andrew Jackson, Nashville, TN: 130

Chester Higgins, Jr./NYT Pictures: 172

Herbert Hoover Presidential Library: 138, 139, 183

Lyndon Baines Johnson Library: ii, 10, 13, 54, 59, 98, 143, 165, 175, 182, 196, 220

Cindy Karp/NYT Pictures: 30

John Fitzgerald Kennedy Library: xi, 5 (top), 7, 26, 83, 85, 158, 160, 194, 198

John Kordell, Metropolitan Singers/Greek Choral Society: 118

Library of Congress: iv, viii, 1, 3, 4, 15, 32, 38, 40, 44, 48, 49, 50, 52, 64, 67, 68, 72, 79, 80, 84, 88, 95, 97, 100, 103, 106, 107, 119, 128, 141 (top), 142, 152, 166, 170, 177, 178, 184, 188, 193, 210

Mount Vernon Ladies Association: 91

Museum of the City of New York: 22, 131, 134, 150

The National Gallery of Art: 181

The New-York Historical Society: 73

Richard Nixon Library & Birthplace: 14, 174, 180★, 197, 204, 212, 221

Nixon Presidential Materials, National Archives: 14, 70, 115, 121

The Pierce Brigade, Concord, NH: 21

Ronald Reagan Presidential Library: vi, xiii, 28, 34, 39, 61, 69, 87, 93, 133, 159, 167, 200

REX, USA, Ltd.: 187

Franklin D. Roosevelt Library: 19, 145, 163, 203, 213

Theodore Roosevelt Collection, Harvard College Library: 9

The Smithsonian Institution: xii, 2, 46, 55, 60, 76, 86, 110, 126,127, 135

Harry S. Truman Library: 35, 65, 122, 132, 137, 223

UPI/Bettmann: xvi, 6, 41, 53, 109, 144, 155

United States Department of the Interior, National Park Service
    Adams National Historic Site: 173
    Sagamore Hill National Historic Site: 189

Wellesley College Archives: 148

White House Historical Association: 43, 90, 92, 104, 105

White House Photo: 208

Woodrow Wilson House/National Trust, Washington, D.C.: x, 81, 141 (bottom), 164, 192, 224


★Big Bird© Jim Henson Productions Inc., courtesy of Children's Television Workshop

# Index

*Page references in italics indicate illustrations.*

Abolition issue, 178. *See also* Civil War
Abortion issue, 64
Adams, Abigail Smith
    biographical information, 207
    drying laundry, *90*
    educational background, 136–137
    as a hostess, 108, 110, 118
    influence on her husband, 74–75, 81
    Jefferson's (Thomas) friendship with,
        180–181
    on living in the White House, 90
    marriage of, 150
    as a mother, 20
    as mother-in-law's caretaker, 27
    as "Mrs. President," xiii
    portrait of, *181*
    post-White House years, 179–181
    relationship with her daughter-in-law, 152
    son's death, 21
Adams, Charles Francis (son of Louisa), 108,
    110, 183
Adams, Charles (son of Abigail), 21
Adams, John, xii, 74–75, 136–137, 150, 180–181
Adams, John Quincy
    on guest list of Monroe's daughter's
        wedding, 15–16
    with his wife, *43*
    marriage of, 152
    on Monroe's (James) borrowing from the
        treasury, 93
    mother's defense of, 20
    wife's lack of influence on, 42
    wife's visits to legislators, 73
Adams, Louisa Catherine Johnson
    biographical information, 207
    with her husband, *43*
    on living in the White House, 42
    marriage of, 152
    portrait of, *173*
    post-White House years, 182–183
    public image of, 171–172
    visits to legislators' wives, 73

Advertisements and First Ladies, 135–136,
    160–161
Advisory role of the First Lady. *See* "Associate
    President" role of the First Lady
Aging, American view on, 132–136
Alcohol consumption, 28–29, 63–64, 129–130,
    162–163, 186. *See also* Prohibition;
    Temperance movement; *specific individuals by
    name*
American Cancer Society, 122
American Heart Association, 122
American Revolution, 40
Anthony, Susan B., 37
Antidrug campaign, 60, *61*
Art Students' League, 58
Arthur, Chester, 42
Arthur, Ellen Lewis Herndon, 207
Artists, women as, 103, *141*, 143
"Associate President" role of the First Lady. *See
    also specific individuals by name*
    advising the president, 74–80
    campaigning behind the scenes, 48–52
    campaigning openly, 52–56
    causes of the First Ladies, 58–62, 119–123
    ceremonial appearances, 65–67
    covering the president's absence, 43–46
    gifts received by First Ladies, 67–69
    "government official" designation of the
        First Lady, 56–58
    guarding access to the president, 46–48
    Monroe's (Elizabeth) rescue mission,
        71–72
    the office of the First Lady gains impor-
        tance, 80–81
    origins of, 39–40
    political activities on the domestic front,
        72–74
    representing the president abroad, 69–71
    running the president's office-residence, 42
    Washington (Martha) sets precedents, 40,
        42
    widening the president's appeal, 63–65

"Aunt Mehitabel." *See* Hazelton, Harriet
Autobiographies and biographies of First Ladies,
    195–202, 215

Bachelor and widowed presidents, 67, 69, 106,
    179
Baldrige, Letitia, xi
*Barbara Bush*, 202
Barbara Bush Foundation for Literacy, 62

## Barbara Bush

The Beach Boys, 119
Beautification and environmental projects, 58,
    *59*, 125, 183. *See also* White House role of
    the First Lady
Begin, Menachem, *66*
*Bess W. Truman*, 198
*Betty—A Glad Awakening*, 186
Betty Ford Center, 186
*The Betty Ford Story*, 186
Biographical information on First Ladies,
    207–214. *See also specific individuals by name*
Biographies and autobiographies of First Ladies,
    195–202, 215
Bloomer, Amelia, 156
Boetigger, John, 20
Boudin, Stephane, 97, 99

Bouvier, Jacqueline. *See* Kennedy, Jacqueline
    Bouvier
Bradwell, Myra, 191
Brico, Antonia, 119
Brook, Edward, *148*
Buchanan, James, 67, 69, 179
Bumbry, Grace, 119
Burial places of First Ladies, 202–204
Bush, Barbara Pierce
    autobiography, 202
    biographical information, 207
    educational background, 149
    with her grandchildren, *169, 201*
    literacy drive, 60, *62*
    personal appearance of, 133, 134, 158
    pet dog, 100, *102*
    photo of, *207*
    post-White House years, 179
    with Reagan (Nancy), *133*
    at Richard Nixon Library dedication, *174*
    at Ronald Reagan Library dedication, *vi*
    at royal White House evening, *82*
    television appearances, 55
    views on significant issues, 154–155, 173
    wedding of, *151*
    at Wellesley's commencement, *146*
    as a woman's advocate, 119
    as a young girl, *216*
Bush, Dorothy, 20
Bush, George
    autobiography, 202
    on broccoli consumption, 115
    with his grandchildren, *201*
    post-White House years, 179
    at Royal White House evening, *82*
    wedding of, *151*
    youthful appearance of, 133
Butt, Archie, 110

Camp David peace talks (1978), 66–67
Camp Fire Girls, 122
Campaigning role of the First Lady, 48–56. *See*
    *also specific individuals by name*
Careers of First Ladies, 141–150, 183–187
Carpenter, Liz, 183
Carson, Rachel, 103
Carter, Amy, *5*

Carter, Billy, 28–29
Carter, Jimmy
    diplomatic ventures of the 1990s, 200–201
    with his grandchildren, *16*
    with his wife and cabinet members, *57*
    wife's campaigning for, 55
    wife's influence on, 75
    wife's representation of abroad, 71
Carter, Rosalynn Smith
    autobiography, 198, 200–201
    biographical information, 207
    Cambodia trip, *71*
    Camp David meeting, *66,* 66–67
    campaigning for her husband, 55
    Caribbean and South America trip, 71
    with Ford (Betty), *199*
    with her daughter, *5*
    with her grandchildren, *16*
    as a hostess, 74, 88, 124
    influence on her husband, 74
    mental health care reform efforts, 57, 58
    photo of, *206*
    with the president and cabinet members,
    *57*
    at Ronald Reagan Library dedication, *vi*
    views on significant issues, 154
    at the White House, *118*
    White House role, 99
    as a wife, 34
    as a woman's advocate, 153
Cassini, Oleg, 158
Causes of the First Lady, 58–62, 119–123. *See*
    *also specific individuals and organizations by*
    *name*
Ceremonial role of the First Lady, 65–67. *See*
    *also specific individuals by name*
Chiang Kai-Shek, Madame, *97*
Childless First Ladies, 2–3
Children of First Ladies, 3–13, 18–27. *See also*
    *specific individuals by name*
Children's Defense Fund, 154
China patterns of the White House, 103–105,
    *105*
Civil rights movement, 55, 79
Civil War, ix, 31, 87, 102–103, 178–179
Clay, Henry, 2
Cleveland, Esther, *8*
Cleveland, Frances Folsom
    biographical information, 208

    with cabinet members' wives, *44*
    with daughters, *8*
    family portrait, *177*
    franking privileges, 189
    gown of, *127*
    as a mother, 6, 8
    pension, 191
    personal appearance of, 135–136
    portrait of, *xii*
    post-White House years, 176
    public deception regarding her husband's
      surgery, 44–46
    on rumors of abuse by her husband, xiii
    sitting for a sculptor, *128*
    temperance stand, 162
Cleveland, Grover, xiii, 6, 8, 44–46, 176, *177*
Cleveland, Ruth, *8*
Clinton, Bill, *xvi,* 55–56, *56*
Clinton, Chelsea, *xvi,* 149
Clinton, Hillary Rodham
    biographical information, 208
    campaigning for her brother, 29–31, *30*
    changing roles of women and, 153, 154
    Clinton administration role, 56–58
    educational background, 147, 149
    on family role of the First Lady, 2
    father's illness, 27
    with her daughter and husband, *xvi*
    with her parents, *27*
    influence on her husband, 81
    with Mitchell (George), *41*
    personal appearance of, 158
    photo of, *208*
    public perception of, xv, 173
    *60 Minutes* appearance, 55–56, *56*
    at the United Nations, *172*
    at Wellesley's commencement in 1969,
      *148*
    in the White House dining room, *116*
    White House furnishing role, 103, 106
Clinton, Roger, 28–29, 31
Community Chest, 122
Confederacy, 31, 178–179. *See also* Civil War
Congressional committees, First Ladies and,
    56–58, 173
Coolidge, Calvin, *24, 25,* 143, 185
Coolidge, Calvin, Jr., 25, 27

**Grace Coolidge**

Coolidge, Grace Goodhue
    after her son's death, *24*
    baking pies, *114*
    biographical information, 208
    educational background, 141, 143, 144
    as a hostess, 123
    with Keller (Helen), *142*
    with military personnel, *186*
    as a mother, 10, 25, 27
    personal appearance of, 155
    pets of, *100, 102*, 102
    portrait of, *96*
    post-White House years, 185–186
    smoking habits, 161
    White House role, 94, 96, 114, 118
    as a wife, 25, 27
    with wounded servicemen, *119*
    as a young girl, *218*
Costs of White House entertaining, 86–89,
    108–111
Cox, Edward, *14*
Custis, Daniel Parke, 17
Custis, John, 17
Custis, Martha Dandridge. *See* Washington,
    Martha Dandridge Custis
Custis, Nelly, 17–18

Dallas, George, 2
Daniel, Margaret Truman, 75, 198
Daughters of the American Revolution, 120
Davis, Edith, *28*
Democratic National Committee
    newsletter, 53
    Women's Division of, 79–80
Depression. *See* The Great Depression
Dewson, Molly, 79–80
Domesticity. *See* Family woman role of the First
    Lady

Earhart, Amelia, 163
Edinburgh, Duke of, *82*
Educational backgrounds of First Ladies,
    136–150
Eisenhower, Dwight, *xiv, 17,* 52, *147,* 197
Eisenhower, Julie Nixon, 15, 197–198
Eisenhower, Mamie Doud
    biographical information, 208
    campaigning for her husband, 52
    causes supported by, 60, 122
    drinking problem allegations, 129–130
    educational background, 136
    with her grandchildren, *17*
    with her husband, *147*
    as a hostess, 119
    illness of, 168
    inaugural gown, 124–125
    personal appearance of, 135
    portrait of, *135, 157*
    press conferences, *51*
    at a public appearance, *xiv*
    in the White House, *112*
    White House role, 89, 113
    on writing an autobiography, 149
Electricity, White House installation of, 117–118
Elizabeth II, Queen of England, *82,* 107–108
Entertaining at the White House, 83–89,
    100–111. *See also specific individuals by name*
Environmental and beautification projects, 58,
    *59,* 125, 183
Expenses of White House entertaining, 86–89,
    108–111

Fall, Albert, 47
Family woman role of the First Lady. *See also*
    *specific individuals by name*
    adult children's careers, 18–21

childless First Ladies, 2–3
deaths of children of First Ladies, 21–27
grandchildren in the White House, 16–18
large families in the White House, 3–4
parents of First Ladies, 27–28
in post-White House years, 179–183
siblings of First Ladies, 28–33
teenagers in the White House, 10–13
views on, 1–2
weddings in the White House, *13, 14,*
    15–16
wife role of the First Lady, 33–37
young children in the White House, 5–10
Farah, Empress of Iran, *83*
Fashion and First Ladies, 124–127, 155–158
Feminism. *See* Role model function of the First
    Lady; Woman's suffrage movement
Ferraro, Geraldine, 154–155
Fillmore, Abigail Powers, *64,* 176, 209
First Ladies' roles
    "Associate President" role, 39–81
    family woman role, 1–37
    in post-White House years, 175–205
    readings on, 215
    role model function, 129–173
    White House role, 88–127
First Lady, Office of the, 80–81
*First Lady from Plains,* 200
"First Lady of the World," *iv*
"First Lady" title, xi
Fisk, Jim, 196
Flowers, Gennifer, 55–56
Folsom, Frances. *See* Cleveland, Frances Folsom
Ford, Elizabeth ("Betty") Bloomer Warren
    biographical information, 209
    with Carter (Rosalynn), *199*
    China trip, *153*
    concession speech for husband, *74*
    educational background, 149–150
    on First Ladies' unpaid role, 192
    with her children, *11*
    on how she will be remembered, 125
    illness of, *168,* 168
    influence on her husband, 74
    as a mother, 12–13
    pet dog, 100
    post-White House years, 175, 186

**Betty Ford**

at press conference, *63*
at Richard Nixon Library dedication, *174*
at Ronald Reagan Library dedication, *vi*
views on significant issues, 154, 172–173
in the White House, *124*
White House staff and, 117
as a woman's advocate, 153
as a young girl, *219*
Ford, Gerald, *74*, 75, 150
Ford, Jack, *11*
Ford, Susan, *11*
Foster Grandparents Program, 60, 166
Franking privileges, 189
French Revolution, 71–72
Fulton, James G., 191–192
Funerals of presidents, First Ladies' presence at, 194–195, 205. *See also* Burial places of First Ladies
Furnishings for the White House, 89–100

Galt, Edith. *See* Wilson, Edith Bolling Galt
Galt, Norman, 203

Gardiner, Julia. *See* Tyler, Julia Gardiner
Garfield, James, 141, 193
Garfield, Lucretia Rudolph, 141, 162, 179, 193, 209
Garfield children, *193*
George VI, King of England, 107–108
Gifts received by First Ladies, 67–69
Girl Scouts, 61, 122
Gold market scandal of 1874, 196
Gorbachev, Raisa, *146*
Gould, Jay, 196
"Government official" designation of First Ladies, 57–58
Gowns of the First Ladies, 124–127
Graber, Ted, 99–100
Grace, Princess of Monaco, 84, *85*
Graham, Martha, 149–150
Grandchildren of First Ladies, 16–18, 179–183. *See also specific individuals by name*
Grant, Julia Dent
  autobiography, 195–196
  biographical information, 209
  daughter's wedding, 16
  with her daughter, *15*
  as a hostess, 87
  on living in the White House, 42
  marriage of, 152
  pension, 191
  portrait of, *88*
  public interest in, ix
Grant, Nellie, *15*, 16
Grant, Ulysses S., 152, 195–196
The Great Depression, 97
Greek Choral Society, *118*
Greenfield, Meg, 71

Habitat for Humanity, 200
Hagerty, James, 123
Hagner, Isabella, 80
"Hail to the Chief," 106
Harding, Florence Kling DeWolfe
  biographical information, 209
  burial site, 203
  campaigning for her husband, 51–52
  departure from the White House, 94
  driving a carriage, *171*
  educational background, 143
  gown of, *126*
  with her husband, *52*

illness of, 170
  marriage of, 152
  pet dog, *101*
  Red Cross boosting by, 60
  transportation preferences, 164
Harding, Warren, 51–52, *52*, 94, 152, 164
Harrison, Anna Symnes, 152, *152*, 189, 209
Harrison, Benjamin, *4*, 191, 203–204
Harrison, Caroline Lavinia Scott
  biographical information, 209
  burial site, 203–204
  causes supported by, 120
  death of, 176
  educational background, 143
  grandchildren of, *4*
  inaugural gown, *127*
  portrait of, *103*
  White House role, 3–4, *103*, 117–118
  as a woman's advocate, 172
Harrison, Mary Scott Dimmick, 191, 204
Harrison, William Henry, 152, 178, 189
Hayes, Lucy Ware Webb
  biographical information, 210
  educational background, 141
  feeding pigeons, *191*
  with friends, *140*
  with her husband and children, *36*
  at her Ohio home, *89*
  as a hostess, 88, 118
  portrait of, *210*
  post-White House years, 196
  public interest in, ix
  temperance stand, 63–64, 162
  travels across the continent, 120
  White House china selection, 102–103, *105*
  as a wife, 34, 36–37
  as a woman's advocate, 172
  Yosemite trip, *120*
Hayes, Rutherford, *36*, *89*, 102
Hazelton, Harriet, 87–88
Health care reform, 56–58, 173
Hearing-impaired persons, work with, 141, 142
Highway beautification and environmental projects, 58, *59*, 125, 183
Hill, George Washington, 160–161

Hoover, Herbert
appointment of women to office, 153
election of, 131
Roosevelt's (Edith) campaigning for, 189
White House staff and, 113–114
wife's campaigning for, 52
wife's relationship with, 138
Hoover, Herbert, Jr., 18
Hoover, Lou Henry
biographical information, 210
campaigning for her husband, 52
causes supported by, 60
driving excursions, 164–165
educational background, 137–138, 144
gift receiving by, 67
with Girl Scouts representatives, *61*
as a grandmother, 18
as a hostess, 73–74
international travels, *139*
meeting with young children, *50*
photography hobby, *183*
portrait of, *138*
radio speeches, 125
White House role, 96, 113–114
as a wife, 37
as a woman's advocate, 153
Hostess role of the First Lady, 73–74, 83–89,
106–111. *See also specific individuals by name*
Housing reform, 58–59

Illnesses of First Ladies, 134, 165–170
Inaugural gowns, 124–127
Infidelity issues, 19, 51, 55–56
Iran, Shah of, *83*

Jackson, Andrew, 117, 129–130
Jackson, Rachel Donelson Robards, 129–130,
*130*, 159, 210
Jaffray, Elizabeth, 111
Jefferson, Martha Wayles Skelton, 210
Jefferson, Thomas, 85, 86, 90, 117, 180–181
Johns Hopkins Medical School, 120, 172
Johnson, Andrew, 75, 166
Johnson, Claudia Alta ("Lady Bird")
autobiography, 133–134, 196, 197
biographical information, 211
campaigning for her husband, 53–55, *54*
as a college student, *143*

**Lady Bird Johnson**

daughter's graduation, *10*
daughter's wedding reception, *13*
daughters' weddings, 15
educational background, 147
environmental and beautification causes,
58, *59*, 125, 183
on family role of the First Lady, 2
with her daughters, *175*
with her grandchildren, *182*
with her grandson, *ii*
Kennedy children's schooling and, 5–6
as a mother, 10, 11–12
with Nixon (Pat), *98*
office of the First Lady and, 81
personal appearance of, 133
post-White House years, 183, *196*
public criticism of, xv
riding a donkey, *165*
at Ronald Reagan Library dedication, *vi*
Truman (Harry) conversations with, 70
White House role, 99, 103, *105*, 116
as a wife, 34
as a young girl, *220*

Johnson, Eliza McCardle, 74, 166, *166*, 211
Johnson, Luci, 12, 15, *175*
Johnson, Lynda
graduation from the University of Texas,
*10*
with her mother, *175*
as a teenager in the White House, 10, 12
wedding of, *13*, 15
Johnson, Lyndon B., 53–55, *184*, 194
"Just Say No" campaign, 60, *61*

Keller, Helen, *142*
Kelly, Grace. *See* Grace, Princess of Monaco
Kennedy, Caroline
as a child in the White House, 5–6
with her father, *37*
at her father's funeral, *194*
with her mother, *6*, 7
with her parents and brother, *xi*, *26*
mother's relationship with, 195
Kennedy, Jacqueline Bouvier
alcohol consumption and social functions,
162–163
assassination and funeral of her husband,
193–195, *194*
biographical information, 211
burial site, 202
campaigning for her husband, 52–53, *53*
educational background, 136
on family role of the First Lady, 2
as a fashion inspiration, *158*, 158
on "First Lady" title, xi
French admiration for, 69
with her daughter Caroline, *6*, 7, *37*
with her granddaughter Rose, *187*
with her husband John and children, *xi*,
*26*
with her son John, *5*
and her son Patrick's death, 27
as a hostess, 87, 119
as "inquiring photographer," *144*
as a mother, 5–6, 195
office of the First Lady and, 80–81
personal appearance of, 136
portrait by Shikler, 124
post-White House years, 186–187
with Reagan (Nancy), *xiii*
smoking habits, 159, *160*

at a state dinner, 83
Truman's (Bess) visit to White House, 198
at a White House lunch, 85
White House role, 58, 89–90, 97, 99, 99, 115–116
Kennedy, John, Jr.
    as a child in the White House, 5–6
    at his father's funeral, 194
    with his mother, 5
    with his parents and sister, xi, 26
    mother's relationship with, 195
Kennedy, John F.
    assassination and funeral, 193–195
    burial site, 202
    with his daughter Caroline, 37
    with his wife and children, xi, 26
    Paris trip, 69
    Roosevelt's (Eleanor) campaigning for, 184
    at a state dinner, 83
    Truman's (Bess) visit to White House, 198
    at a White House lunch, 85
    wife's campaigning for, 53
    with Wilson (Edith), 192

Lafayette, Marquise de, 71–72
Lane, Harriet, 67, 67, 69
Lansing (Secretary of State under Wilson), 47
Lash, Joseph, 69, 184
Latrobe, Benjamin, 90–91
Laxalt, Paul, 77
Leadership of women by the First Lady. See
    Role model function of the First Lady
Legal Services Corporation, 154
Lighthouse for the Blind, 122
Lincoln, Abraham, 22, 166, 189–190, 195
Lincoln, Edward, 22–23
Lincoln, Mary Todd
    biographical information, 211
    competitiveness with other women, 154
    family portrait, 22
    family's Civil War loyalties, 31
    as a hostess, 87, 107
    party given by, 86
    pensions and other public compensations, 179, 189–191
    portrait of, 188

public interest in, ix
sons' deaths, 22–23, 25
White House furnishing role, 93–94
Lincoln, Robert, 190
Lincoln, Tad, 22, 190
Lincoln, Willie, 22, 23, 25
Literacy drive, 60, 62, 63
Lodge, Henry Cabot, 47
Long, Ava, 114
Longworth, Alice Roosevelt, 8–10, 16, 93, 111

MacLean, Evalyn, 161
Madison, Dorothea ("Dolley") Payne Todd
    biographical information, 211
    burial site, 203
    educational background, 140
    and First Lady play, xi
    as a hostess, 84–86, 123
    as Orphans' Asylum directress, 119
    pet macaw, 102
    popularity of, 72–73
    portrait of, 73, 84
    post-White House years, 181–182
    Van Buren (Angelica) relationship to, 106–107
    White House furnishing role, 90–91
Madison, James, xi, 72–73, 181
Manchester, William, 194
Mangione, Jerre, 78
March of Dimes, 60, 122
Marcos, Ferdinand, 77
Marcos, Imelda, 77
Marriage patterns of First Ladies, 150–153
McCaffree, Mary, 80
McKim, Charles, 94
McKinley, Ida Saxton
    biographical information, 211
    brother's murder, 31–33
    competitiveness with other women, 154
    illness of, 168–170, 170
    photo on campaign buttons, 55
    portrait of, 32, 170
Meir, Golda, 162
Mental health care reform, 57, 58
Mercer, Lucy, 19
Merry, Anthony, 85–86
Mitchell, George J., 41
Mitterand, François, 155
Mondale, Walter, 154

Monroe, Elizabeth Kortright
    avoidance of visits to legislators' wives, 73
    biographical information, 211
    daughter's wedding, 15–16
    marriage of, 150, 152
    portrait of, 72, 92
    rescue of the Marquise de Lafayette, 71–72
    spending habits, 110
    White House Monroe suite and, 96
    White House role, 91–93, 105
Monroe, James, 91–93, 92, 96, 110, 117
Monroe, Maria, 15–16
Motherhood and First Ladies, 3–13, 18–27. See
    also specific individuals by name
"Mrs. President," xiii
My Turn, 201

Nancy Reagan Foundation, 201
Napoleon, Prince of France, 107
National Foundation for Infantile Paralysis, 122
National themes in the White House, 102–106
National Wildflower Research Center, 183
Nesbitt, Henrietta, 114
New York Metropolitan Singers, 118
Nixon, Julie. See Eisenhower, Julie Nixon

**Pat Nixon**

Nixon, Patricia ("Pat") Ryan
    biographical information, 212
    biography of, 197–198

campaigning for her husband, 52–53
causes supported by, 122–123
daughters' weddings, *14*, 15, 16
educational background, 147
with her grandchildren, *180*
with Johnson (Lady Bird), *98*
personal appearance of, 134, 156
photo of, *212*
popularity after leaving the White House,
   xii, xv
at Richard Nixon Library dedication, *174*
at Ronald Reagan Library dedication, *vi*
smoking habits, 162
western Africa trip, *70*
at the White House, *115*, *121*, *197*
White House role, 99
as a young girl, *221*
Nixon, Richard, *14*, 75, 134, 197, *205*
Nixon, Tricia, *14*, 15
Novak, William, 201
Nureyev, Rudolph, 187

Office of the First Lady, 80–81
Office of the President, 42
Onassis, Aristotle, 186, 202
Onassis, Jacqueline Kennedy. *See* Kennedy,
   Jacqueline Bouvier
Orphans' Asylum, 119

Parents of First Ladies, 27–28. *See also specific*
   *individuals by name*
*Pat Nixon: The Untold Story*, 197–198
Pearce, Lorraine, 97
Pensions and other public compensations, 179,
   189–192
Perkins, Frances, 131
Personal appearance standards for First Ladies,
   132–136
Pets in the White House, xi, 100–102
Pierce, Barbara. *See* Bush, Barbara Pierce
Pierce, Benjamin, *21*, 22
Pierce, Franklin, 21–22
Pierce, Jane Means Appleton, *21*, 21–22, 212
Political role of the First Lady. *See* "Associate
   President" role of the First Lady
Polk, James, *2*, 2, 75

Polk, Sarah Childress
   biographical information, 212
   educational background, 138, 140
   on family role of the First Lady, 2–3
   with her husband, *2*
   influence on her husband, 74, 81
   post-White House years, *178*, 179
   White House role, 117
Portraits of First Ladies, 124–125. *See also specific*
   *individuals by name*
Post-White House role of the First Lady
   burial places of First Ladies, 202–204
   careers and life changes, 183–187
   duration of the post-Washington years,
      176–179
   former First Ladies on, 175, 204–205
   grandmothering and gardening, 179–183
   pensions and other public compensations,
      189–192
   public interest in former First Ladies,
      193–195
   writing about their lives, 184, 195–202
Presidency. *See also specific individuals by name*
   constitutional guidelines for, 40, 42
   salary of the president, 108
Presidential china, 103–105, *105*
Press conferences, *51*, *62*, 123–124, *156*
Preston, Frances Cleveland, 189. *See also*
   Cleveland, Frances Folsom
Preston, Thomas Jex, 176
Prohibition, 124, 161, 162. *See also* Temperance
   movement
Public access to the White House, 123–124
Public perceptions of First Ladies, ix–xv, 63–65,
   129–132, 165–170. *See also specific individuals*
   *by name*

Radio speeches by First Ladies, 125
Rainier, Prince of Monaco, *85*
Rather, Dan, 77
Reagan, Nancy Davis
   on *Air Force One*, *39*
   autobiography, 201–202
   biographical information, 212
   with Bush (Barbara), *133*
   expansion of the First Lady role by, 39–40
   Gridiron dinner appearance, *159*
   with her husband, *34*, *167*, *200*
   with her mother, *28*

as a hostess, 88–89, 108
illness of, 166–168
influence on her husband, 75, 76–78
"Just Say No" campaign, 60, *61*
Mexico City trip, *69*
mother's death, 28
with Onassis (Jacqueline Kennedy), *xiii*
at Paris dinner, *155*
personal appearance of, 134, 155, 158
pet dog, 100
at Ronald Reagan Library dedication, *vi*
television appearances, 55
in the White House, *87*, *93*
White House role, 99–100, 103, *105*, 117
as a wife, 34
Reagan, Ronald
   aboard *Air Force One*, *39*
   with his wife, *34*, *167*, *200*
   wife's devotion to, 201–202
   wife's influence on, 75, 76–78
Red Cross, 60, 122
Regan, Donald, 76–77
Reno, Janet, 154
Robb, Charles, 183
Rodham, Dorothy, *27*
Rodham, Hillary. *See* Clinton, Hillary Rodham
Rodham, Hugh, Jr., 29–31, *30*
Rodham, Hugh, Sr., *27*, 27
Rodham, Tony, 31
Role model function of the First Lady
   changing roles of women and, 153–155
   clothing styles and costs, 155–158
   educational backgrounds of First Ladies,
      136–150
   illnesses of First Ladies and public percep-
      tions, 165–170
   marriage patterns of First Ladies, 150–153
   personal appearance standards for First
      Ladies, 132–136
   public affairs arena, 171–173
   public perceptions and, 129–132
   smoking and drinking preferences of First
      Ladies, 159–163
   transportation preferences of First Ladies,
      163–165
Roosevelt, Alice. *See* Longworth, Alice
   Roosevelt

Roosevelt, Anna, 20–21
Roosevelt, Anna Eleanor
    with African American supporters, 79
    air travel by, 163, 163
    biographical information, 213
    burial site, 204
    campaigning by, 29, 48, 52, 184
    congressional committee appearance by,
        57
    defense of Smith (Katie), 131
    driving excursions, 165
    at Easter egg roll, 123
    educational background, 144, 146
    family portrait, 19
    as "First Lady of the World," iv
    with her husband, 145, 213
    as a hostess, 73–74, 107–108, 119
    influence on her husband, 78–80, 81, 172
    with Madame Chiang Kai-Shek, 97
    as a mother, 1–2, 20–21
    personal appearance of, 156
    portrait of, 109
    post-White House years, 184–185
    press conferences of, 123–124, 156
    public criticism of, xv
    radio speeches, 125
    smoking habits, 161–162
    South Pacific trip, 38, 68, 69–70, 122
    visiting servicemen abroad, 129
    White House role, 96–97, 103, 114
    as a wife, 33–34
    as a woman's advocate, 153
Roosevelt, Archie, 9, 9–10
Roosevelt, Dorothy Kemp, 29
Roosevelt, Edith Kermit Carow
    biographical information, 213
    burial site, 204
    campaigning for Hoover, 189
    First Lady's office and, 80–81
    with her son Quentin, 110
    as a hostess, 110–111, 118
    influence on her husband, 80
    as a mother, 8–10
    pension, 191
    personal appearance of, 156
    portrait gallery and, 124
    portrait of, 80, 95

    stepdaughter's wedding, 16
    White House role, 94, 118
Roosevelt, Ethel, 9
Roosevelt, Franklin D.
    appointment of women to office, 153
    death of, 133
    family portrait, 19
    with his wife, 145, 213
    pet dog, 100
    socializing of, 161
    White House staff and, 114
    wife's influence on, 78–80, 172
    wife's refusal to campaign for, 52
Roosevelt, Quentin, 8–10, 9, 110
Roosevelt, Sara Delano, 33
Roosevelt, Theodore, 8–10, 9, 50, 80, 204
Roosevelt, Theodore, Jr., 8–10, 9
Rutledge, Ann, 190

Sadat, Anwar-al, 66
Saint-Gaudens, Augustus, 128
Salaries
    for presidents, 108
    proposed for president's wives, 191–192
Salinger, Pierre, 5
Saxton, George, 31–33
Shalala, Donna, 154
Siblings of First Ladies, 28–33. See also specific
    individuals by name

60 Minutes, 55–56, 56
Smith, Alfred E., 130–132, 131
Smith, Catherine "Katie" Dunn, 130–132, 131
Smith, Robert, 72–73
Smith, William, 150
Smoking habits, 159–162
Staff of the White House, 112–117. See also spe-
    cific individuals by name
Stanton, Elizabeth, 37
Story, Joseph, 140

Taft, Helen Herron
    autobiography, 196
    biographical information, 213
    with her daughter, 48
    with her husband, 49
    as a hostess, 111
    and husband's election and administration,
        48–51
    illness of, 170
    outfit of, 126
    pension, 191
    White House staff and, 112
Taft, William Howard, 48–51, 49, 80, 122
Tarbell, Ida, 131
Task Force on Health Care Reform, 56–58, 173
Taylor, Margaret Mackall Smith, xv, 159–160,
    213
Taylor, Zachary, 160
Teenagers in the White House, 10–13. See also
    specific individuals by name
Television appearances by First Ladies, 55–56,
    56
Temperance movement, 162. See also
    Prohibition
Templesman, Maurice, 187
Thomas, Helen, 162
Todd, Dolley Payne. See Madison, Dorothea
    ("Dolley") Payne Todd
Transportation preferences of First Ladies,
    163–165
Truman, Elizabeth Virginia ("Bess") Wallace
    alcohol consumption, 163
    biographical information, 214
    biography of, 198
    causes supported by, 60, 122
    christening an airplane, 65, 65–66
    educational background, 143–144

**Bess Truman**

epitaph, 204
family portrait, *35*
with her husband, *132*
inaugural gown, 125
influence on her husband, 75
Kennedy White House visit by, *198*
marriage of, 152–153
as mother's caretaker, 28
personal appearance of, 133
on tennis court, *137*
on "whistle-stop" tour, *76*
White House role, 103, 114–115, 118
with a White House visitor, *122*
as a wife, 34
as a young girl, *223*
Truman, Harry S
    appointment of Roosevelt (Eleanor) as
        UN delegate, 185
    on criticisms of his wife's appearance, 133
    family portrait, *35*
    with his wife, *132*
    Johnson (Lady Bird) conversations with,
        70
    marriage of, 152–153
    on "whistle-stop" tour, *76*
    White House changes during administra-
        tion of, 97
    wife's epitaph, 204
    wife's influence on, 75
Truman, Margaret. *See* Daniel, Margaret Truman
Turnure, Pamela, 81
Tyler, John, 3, 176
Tyler, Julia Gardiner
    biographical information, 214
    as a hostess, 106
    portrait of, *106, 107*
    posing for advertisement, *134*, 135
    post-White House years, 176, 178–179
Tyler, Letitia Christian, 3, 176, 214
Tyler, Priscilla Cooper, 3, *3*

United Nations, *172*, 185

Van Buren, Angelica, *87*, 106–107
Van Buren, Hannah Hoes, 214
Van Buren, Martin, 106
Vandenberg, Arthur, 185
Verdon, René, 115–116

Wallace, Madge, 152–153
War of 1812, 91
Washington, George, 40–44, 67, 91, 150
Washington, Martha Dandridge Custis
    biographical information, 214
    burial site, 203
    covering the president's absence, 43–44
    franking privileges, 189
    gift receiving by, 67
    as a grandmother, 16–18
    marriage of, 150
    portrait of, *viii, 40, 91, 150*
    precedents set by, 40, 42
    public image of, ix, 171
    running the president's office-residence, 42
Webb, Lucy. *See* Hayes, Lucy Ware Webb
Weddings in the White House, *13, 14,* 15–16
Welk, Lawrence, 119
West, J. B., *98,* 113, 134, 163
*A White House Diary*, 133–134, 196, 197
White House role of the First Lady. *See also spe-*
    *cific individuals by name*
    charitable drives and the White House,
        119–123
    china pattern selections, 103–105
    exhibition of portraits and gowns,
        124–127
    furnishings for the nation's house, 89–100
    hostess responsibilities, 84–89, 106–108
    national themes in the White House,
        102–106
    paying the bills, 108–111
    pets in the White House, xi, 100–102
    public access to the White House,
        123–124
    responsibility for the mansion, 117–118
    significance of, 83–84
    staffing issues, 112–117
    views on, 42
    weddings in the White House, *13, 14,*
        15–16
Wife role of the First Lady, 33–37. *See also spe-*
    *cific individuals by name*
Wilson, Edith Bolling Galt
    autobiography, 196–197
    biographical information, 214
    burial site, 203
    driving excursions, 163–164, *164*
    Europe trip, *x, 81*

## Edith Wilson

    franking privileges, 189
    with her husband, *46*
    influence on her husband, 46–48
    with Kennedy (John), *192*
    post-White House years, 193
    White House china display room by, *104*
    as a young girl, *219*
Wilson, Eleanor, *224*
Wilson, Ellen Axson
    biographical information, 214
    burial site, 202
    daughters' weddings, 16
    death of, 176
    educational background, 143
    with her daughters, *1*
    housing reform efforts, 58–59
    painting by, *141*
    personal appearance of, 156, 158
    portrait of, *141*
Wilson, Jessie, *1*
Wilson, Woodrow, *46,* 46–48, *81,* 156, 202–203
Woman's suffrage movement, 37, 172
Women's Christian Temperance Union, 63–64
Women's roles and First Ladies, 129–173
World War I, 47, 73–74, 161
World War II, 69–70, 97, 122, 165, 185
Wright, Zephyr, 116

Youth, American emphasis on, 132–136

Martha Dandridge Custis Washington 1789-1797 ⋆ Abigail Sm

⋆ Elizabeth Kortright Monroe 1817-1825 ⋆ Louisa Catherine

Letitia Christian Tyler 1841-1842 ⋆ Julia Gardine

⋆ Margaret Mackall Smith Taylor 1849-1850 ⋆ Abigail Powe

Mary Todd Lincoln 1861-1865 ⋆ Eliza McCard

⋆ Lucy Webb Hayes 1877-1881 ⋆ Lucretia Rudolph Garfiel

Caroline Scott Harrison 1889-1892 ⋆ Ida Saxton

⋆ Helen Herron Taft 1909-1913 ⋆ Ellen Axson Wil

Florence Kling Harding 1921-1923 ⋆ Grace Goodhu

⋆ Eleanor Roosevelt Roosevelt 1933-1945 ⋆ Bess Wallace

Jacqueline Bouvier Kennedy 1961-1963 ⋆ Lady Bird I

⋆ Betty Bloomer Warren Ford 1974-1977 ⋆ Rosalynn

Barbara Pierce Bush 1989-1993 ⋆ Hillary Rodha